NEW AGE

M U S I C I A N S

NEW AGE MUSICIANS

Edited By Judie Eremo

From the pages of Guitar Player, Keyboard, and Frets magazines

GPI Publications
Cupertino, California

ISBN 0-88188-909-1

Hal Leonard Publishing Corporation

7777 West Bluemound Road, Milwaukee, WI 53213

GPI BOOKS

Director
Alan Rinzler

Editor: *New Age Musicians*
Judie Eremo

Art Director
Paul Haggard

Art Assistant
Robert Stockwell Jr.

Proofreader
Spot Cichon

Assistant
Marjean Wall

GPI PUBLICATIONS

President/Publisher
Jim Crockett

Executive Vice President
Don Menn

Corporate Art Director
Wales Christian Ledgerwood

Production
Cheryl Matthews (Director)
Joyce Phillips (Assistant Director)
Andrew Gordon, Gail M. Hall, Joe Verri

Typesetting
Leslie K. Bartz (Director)
Pat Gates, June Ramirez

Marketing
Tim Bardel
Nelson Cooney
Perry Fotos
Lynn Slade

Accounting
Thomas E. Murphy (Director)
Rekha Shah
Lynne Whitlach

Photo Credits

Cover photo: Courtesy of NASA.
Cover design: Paul Haggard
Page 9: Irene Young; 19: 23: Jon Sievert; 30: Mark Mander; 47: Ann
Summa; 73: Ebet Roberts; 78: Jon Sievert; 95: Tim Davis; 102: Jon
Sievert; all others courtesy of artists.

ISBN: 0-88188-909-1

CONTENTS

INTRODUCTION

By Bob Doerschuk

Keyboard, October 1988

New age means exactly that . . . A new age. New possibilities, not just in music, but in life. No more fear. No more war. No more bebop runs or flat 9th chords. Humanity could drift toward enlightenment on clouds of synthesized fifths, or float heavenward amidst pentatonic chimes, whose tinkling would sparkle like soft rain amidst the silence of the spheres.

It seems like a perfect tonic for an ailing planet. After surviving drugs, Vietnam, and the trauma of lost innocence, an entire generation was staggering toward adulthood, desperate for healing. The outcome is the music of Tony Scott, Steven Halpern, Paul Horn, Kitaro, and George Winston. The music became a movement, beginning as a ripple, gently stirring shoppers in health food stores and book shops. Gradually it rose to a higher tide, lapping the summit of Windham Hill, coursing down the aisles of mainstream record stores and cresting on dozens of radio playlists. Suddenly, America was listening. Soothing itself in warm showers of sound.

So new age is happening. It's now. And, for that very reason, it's not new age anymore. Unlike most styles recognized by the Grammy gurus, new age and the music industry don't mix at the most basic philosophical levels. Classical music rests on Western concepts of order and control; rock and jazz infuse these concepts with neo-African exultation. Pop music as a whole is about celebrating one system or another. The successes of Journey, David Sanborn, and each new wave of piano competition winners testify to the health of our culture's musical and cultural machinery.

Not so with new age. Back in 1964, when Tony Scott released *Music For Zen Meditation,* he was saying, in effect, "We live in times so twisted that we need to escape them for our own good. We need music that doesn't catapult you up and down predictable structures. In a society that emphasizes competition, this album is passive. Rather than try to carve each other like bloodthirsty boppers, these musicians improvise cooperatively. They prefer a peaceful stasis to a headlong scramble from cadence to cadence."

Music For Zen Meditation was subversive. It existed because Scott saw problems at the root of Western society, and concluded that music could help listeners deal with them only by going outside of our system of artistic and ethical values. Like the minimalists, who followed a curiously parallel path, the new age pioneers defined themselves in terms of what was wrong with their world, and what they could do to fix things.

Steven Halpern, one of the most influential leaders of the early new age movement, explained his musical approach in a recent issue of *Prevention:* "The foundation of Western music, especially classical, is one of tension and release. As a passage steadily builds in intensity, your anticipation level builds with it. You're waiting for the big payoff, the release. But when the climax finally comes, the tension starts building all over again . . . at a higher level."

Halpern's solution was to create a new type of music, free of the stress that's built into even the most mellow mainstream styles. Implicit in his exploration was a criticism of Western beliefs, at least as far as using music to heal fractured psyches is concerned. Though these ideas appealed to many people, others took umbrage at suggestions that their values were bankrupt, and possibly even harmful.

Though Halpern is a significant figure in new age music, he was hardly the first to ruffle the establishment's feathers. While he was performing before projections of mandalas in the San Francisco Bay area during the mid-'70s, a German composer/synthesist named Peter Michael Hamel was attacking Western preconceptions in his influential book, *Through Music To The Self.* Hamel's defense of drugs, including LSD, as catalysts to musical mind expansion only made the proto-new age movement more controversial:

"The musical LSD trip was able to help many a previously mindless note-spinner to achieve a pitch of self-knowledge that was to influence his whole subsequent output. A prolonged note would be heard across a new and much greater range of overtones. . . . Suffused by an overpowering sense of joy, one could submerge oneself in one's music, experience a grace and an almost holy awe. With other musicians one felt a marvelous oneness, while retaining nevertheless the feeling of one's own identity amidst the whole. This experience, which one could almost call mystical, culminated in spontaneous, deep insights into the relationship of man to the world of sounds."

In the past decade, since the appearance of Hamel's book, psychedelics have lost their allure. But the new age movement continues to bear a stigma. Like the fabled hippies of the '60s, its adherents pursue meaning outside of rationality. Their quasi-mystical doctrines draw potshots from nightclub comics and Christian apocalyptics. And their music, with its resolute simplicity and invitation to passivity, still drives critics—and unconverted musicians—crazy.

In analyzing George Winston's new age piano style, Keith Jarrett said in *Musician*, "The implications of his music are interesting, because it's used for meditating, for relaxing, for falling asleep, for having conversations during—the exact opposite of my reasons for playing. If someone can fall asleep or meditate while the music is going on, to me that's spiritually not right."

Yet many new age devotees cite Jarrett's solo piano improvisations as milestones in the development of their musical consciousness. Though Jarrett may bristle, his *Köln Concert* and many other '70s-vintage ECM albums have surfaced on new age playlists. So have Tomita's electronic variations on Western classical themes. And pop hits, including Mike Oldfield's *Tubular Bells*. And Philip Glass' busy minimalist adventures. Even John Coltrane's late free improvisations have been appropriated by some more creative new age programmers.

So what gives? What is new age music, anyway? Can we define it in musical terms? Is it simply a gimmick hatched by the industry's marketing wizards? Or does it boil down to something more ephemeral—spiritual essence, say, or the performer's method, or the positive ion count in the recording studio?

In tracking down a definition of new age music, we thought we'd start, logically enough, with *The New Age Dictionary*, published in 1976 and now out of print. Here, we learned that new age is "a movement devoted to making Earth a happy place to live, of Sufis, yogis, shamans, native Americans, macrobiotics, Theosophists, organic farmers, peace activists, environmentalists, alternative energy people, particle physicists, radical educators, holistic healers, human potentialists, psy-

chotronics and physical investigators . . ." Not a word about whether 16-bar structure or diatonic harmony fits into the scheme.

So we took the next best step, and checked out what some of the musicians identified with the movement had to say. Unfortunately, though much of what we encountered evoked vivid images, it left us equally unenlightened: George Winston talks about "sound incense." Eddie Jobson, whose solo piano recordings on Private Music earn him a place on new age playlists, suggests that this style is a "soundtrack for the movie of the mind." Andreas Vollenweider, winner of the first Grammy for Best New Age Recording, calls it "space to work with, space to use, space with no danger. With this music, you can build a bridge between conscious and subconscious."

Hmmm. Not much to work with here. Maybe a musicology doctoral candidate in search of a dissertation could straighten all this out. Until we hear from them, however, our vote for the most authoritative view of the subject goes to Suzanne Doucet, president of Beyond Records, founder of the New Age Music Network, owner of the Only New Age Music store in Hollywood, and an outspoken enthusiast for this style.

"First of all, new age music is instrumental," she insists. "This is because instrumental music bypasses the intellectual center, going directly to the right half of the brain, which is more intuitive and imaginative than the left half. It has something in common with jazz, in that both styles are improvisational. But jazz is not designed to relax; instead, it builds up tension toward a climax. New age music is the opposite. It relaxes and heals. You can expand your consciousness simply by listening to it."

Doucet adds that the phenomenal success of this style has triggered a crisis. In a recent issue of *Billboard*, she warned that "the popularity of new age music presents quite a paradox. The irony of the push for its economic success becomes apparent when one examines its original purpose, which is to slow down the listener, to relax, balance, and heal. . . . In direct contrast, almost every success-oriented business, including the music industry, operates by overstimulating and exciting the intellect and the senses, focusing on performance and personality, concerning itself with numbers rather than quality. New age music, now a major part of the music industry, has become subject to the disease it was trying to heal."

In Doucet's view, the impact of new age on pop

music must therefore be analyzed in spiritual as well as musical terms. But, she acknowledges, the commercial corruption of the new age theology also brings musicians face-to-face with economic questions. "If you don't have a well-defined product, you cannot do the right marketing," Doucet insists. "All the major companies who are distributing new age labels are frustrated because the music is not selling as well as they wanted it to. The major mistake they made is in marketing. You can't market real new age like pop music or jazz or classical."

Stephen Hill, host of the radio program *Music From The Hearts Of Space*, agrees that the interests of new age purists and music industry hustlers seldom intersect. "One of the healthy things about the new age genre is that it took the emphasis off of the virtuoso tradition in music," he points out. "But as soon as you get record companies trying to maximize their sales by pumping up their artists and sending them out for live performances, you're back to virtuosity, performance values, charisma, and all that other stuff that focuses on the individual artist. Although some incredibly fine work is still being done, there has been a dilution of the original intentions."

It's happened before: Songs sung to spark rebellion are now co-opted for the greater glory of selling beer or shoes. But the growth of adult contemporary music is perhaps an even greater misfortune. Ripping off new age is like taking a balloon from a child. Musical devices once embraced by visionary innocents as tools of self-discovery have been cynically seized by fading superstars scrambling for air time, or misused by technical primitives incapable of surviving without sequencers. Of course, pure new age artistry lives on, played by gifted and tenacious musicians. Though some of them may disavow the label, they are new-agers nonetheless, and should be proud of it. Those who persist in pursuing enlightenment through music deserve our admiration.

But, sadly, the day of these hardy idealists seems to have passed. Nowadays even Lee Abrams, whose concept of tight radio formatting helped destroy progressive radio, is in the new age ball game as president of Cinema Records. "This music appeals to two types of people," Abrams told *Christianity Today*. "First, to those who grew up with progressive rock in the '60s and early '70s . . . . Second, to the person who likes nice atmospheric music to relax to, but finds Mantovanni awfully old and boring." Surprise! New age has made the leap from spiritual to demographic phenomenon. The feel and sound of this music continues to exert a wide influence.

*   *   *   *

NEW AGE MUSICIANS contains articles reprinted from *Guitar Player, Keyboard,* and *Frets* magazines. Magazine names with dates of issue are listed at the beginning of each article.

The Musicians

PHILIP AABERG

By Jim Aikin

Keyboard, April 1986

Some tunes you have to sweat blood over. A melody that ends up sounding simple and natural may have been nailed down one note at a time. Other times, a melody comes to you whole, and says, "Play me." Trying to complicate it after the fact only takes you further away from the inspiration.

"High Plains," the title track of Philip Aaberg's recent solo piano album, is a tune that arrived in one piece, needing only the most transparent of arrangements. "The hard part," Aaberg confides, "was keeping it simple through the rest of the piece. I could have taken the tune as the opening of an improvisation, but that didn't seem to work out. I always had to come back to playing the main theme."

Part of the trick, of course, is to have a well enough developed musical consciousness that when such a tune arrives, you can recognize it and get a secure grip on it before it floats away again. Aaberg's highly varied background gave him the best possible preparation for this. While attending Harvard, he both studied classical piano and played in a succession of off-campus bands, including one that specialized in New Orleans jazz. After a stint playing chamber music at the Marlboro Chamber Festival, he moved to the West Coast and started hanging out in blues clubs.

Before long, he had joined forces with guitarist Elvin Bishop. "Elvin asked me to join his band," Aaberg reports. "I made six albums with him, and toured with him for a year and a half. After that, I taught for a while at the East Bay Center for the Arts, in Richmond, California, which provides low-cost lessons for kids who might not otherwise be able to have music lessons." He has since toured with vocalists Peter Gabriel and Maria Muldaur and former Doobie Brothers guitarist Tom Johnson, and recorded five albums with Juice Newton.

In spite of such diverse leanings, it might seem odd that Aaberg chose the new age acoustic piano style for his first solo album. As with the melody of "High Plains," the opportunity more or less fell into his lap.

"I had been writing for a long time," he explains, "but I couldn't find the right vehicle for what I did. At one point I said, 'I'm going to stop doing studio work and work for a year on my own stuff, and if nothing happens I'll become a mailman.' I wasn't too aware of Windham Hill Records at the time, but the very next day, a friend of mine told me that he had spoken to them about me, and that they wanted to hear a demo."

Most of the artists working in the folk piano idiom use the same basic vocabulary of keyboard devices, so it's tempting to suppose that they all listen to one another and cop licks. Not so, insists Aaberg. "I purposely didn't listen to [Windham Hill pianists] George Winston or Liz Story," he says. "If I sounded like them I didn't want to be influenced by them, and if I didn't sound like them I didn't want to try to sound like them at all."

The entire *High Plains* [Windham Hill, 1037], album took only four days to record, and a good deal of that time was spent on microphone placement. Aaberg relied on placement to get the sound he wanted; he reports that there is no processing or equalization on the recording at all. A Hamburg Steinway C was used, and he insists that the C, at 7'4", is better for recording than the 9' D. "The 9' grand is very good for putting out a lot of sound when you're in a big hall," he indicates, "and cutting through an orchestra. But it's not as even along the whole range as the smaller pianos. You have to mike it from a long distance away. I think that's why a lot of classical recordings sound like you're out in the audience, when it might be more effective to be close."

Only the first half of "High Plains" is transcribed here, and that in a slightly abbreviated form. After stating the melody three times, Aaberg goes into a B section (beginning at the double bar, bar 265) in which a chord progression alternates with a banjo-like figure. This section occurs three times in succession, with enough minor variations in rhythm and chord voicing that simple repeat marks wouldn't accurately represent the performance. Due to limitations of

space, however, we couldn't transcribe all three run-throughs of the material. So we have compromised by giving the first statement of the chordal phrase, followed immediately by the third instance of the banjo figure. If you have the record, you should be able to reconstruct the full section easily; if not, feel free to improvise something appropriate with this material before returning to the melody as shown. After another short interlude, Aaberg restates the melody at double length, slowing it down and adding passing tones, before winding up with another statement of the unaccompanied original.

The modal simplicity of the melody allows for many different harmonizations. Aaberg makes use of several progressions, all of them within the boundaries of diatonic harmony; as you play the piece, you may discover other possibilities for yourself. The eight-bar melody comprising four two-bar phrases is standard in folk music, but a more usual progression would go to the dominant (or some other chord) at the end of the third phrase. When Aaberg slides down to a root-position tonic chord here (the third bar back from the end of the transcription), he creates a striking sense of response. The final phrase, while rounding out the structure, is transformed into a kind of echo. This is the sort of touch, easy to analyze but tough to find on the keyboard, that makes the difference between the pedestrian and the inspired in the understated world of new age piano. □

"High Plains"

By Philip Aaberg

etc.

WILL ACKERMAN

By Dan Forte

Guitar Player, February 1985

The year is 1979, and Will Ackerman is throwing a party at the Music Annex recording studio in Menlo Park, California. The occasion is the release of his third album of acoustic guitar pieces, *Childhood And Memory,* on his own label, Windham Hill Records. Old friends munch and chat while the Pat Metheny Group's "Phase Dance" blasts over the monitors. The song is interrupted and a toast is proposed—not with champagne, but with music. Bill Quist (who is working on an album of Erik Satie compositions for the label) takes a seat at the Steinway and unfolds a manuscript as Ackerman looks on like a wide-eyed child. An unabashed grin overtakes the guitarist's face as Quist coaxes a note-perfect arrangement of Ackerman's best-known composition, "The Bricklayer's Beautiful Daughter," from the ivories.

* * * *

That rendition said more about Will Ackerman, guitarist/composer, than it did Bill Quist, pianist/arranger. Any number of his acoustic guitar solos could sound at home on a keyboard or any other melodic instrument—a fact that clearly separates him from the "American primitive" (John Fahey, Leo Kottke, Robbie Basho) and British folk (Bert Jansch, John Renbourn, Davey Graham) schools that defined "steel-string guitar" before Ackerman came along. (It would be hard to imagine a piano arrangement of a typical Kottke composition, for instance, because of its idiomatic nature.)

Will Ackerman didn't father a new genre, but if any player typifies the new generation of fingerstyle steel-stringers, it's the 35-year-old ex-carpenter. Not only does his own style (however rooted in Fahey and Basho) have its own distinct personality, but as a record company executive, he built a mini-empire largely on young, unknown acoustic guitarists. Inasmuch as Ackerman's taste was the sole barometer of what the label did or didn't record, he handpicked the starting lineup for much of the team that makes up this so-called new school.

Windham Hill isn't the only breeding ground for new age phenoms, but it is by far the most visible and successful. It got its start when friends asked Ackerman to tape them some of his original guitar pieces back in 1975, resulting in his debut album, *Turtle's Navel.* Will began finding other acoustic guitarists that he wanted to record, and an extremely loyal audience began relying on his taste to provide an audiophile-quality, mostly laid-back alternative to commercial radio. In 1980, Ackerman produced *Autumn,* a collection of sound paintings by pianist George Winston. That album and Winston's *December* have since gone gold (sales in excess of 500,000). Initial orders for the *Windham Hill Records Sampler '84* LP were over 100,000 units. In September '84 alone, the label sold approximately 300,000 units of various titles. "At this point, a halfway reasonable budget on any new album puts us in the black on initial orders," Ackerman beams. "We have never lost money on a single project." At the time of this writing, the label had six LPs on *Billboard's* Pop chart; it has placed as many as nine albums simultaneously on the magazine's Jazz chart. Not surprisingly, Will Ackerman was named as one of the "men and women under 40 who are changing America" in *Esquires's 1984 Register: The Best Of The New Generation.*

"Windham Hill music" has been described as lyrical, pastoral, meditative, and romantic. Its detractors have called it "hot tub Muzak" and "non-music for non-musicians." While he insists that there is no style or category that sums up the label—citing artists as far flung as Michael Hedges, trumpet/synthesist Mark Isham, and pianist Liz Story—it is difficult even for Ackerman not to lapse into discussing the label and the music interchangeably: "We didn't set out to create any genre of music. The fact that we're maybe the most visible collection of it in the world right now makes people refer to it as 'Windham Hill.' And, of course, the retailers have established Windham Hill bins, and there

is that sort of loyalty in the record buying public. We really have never been static, despite the fact that people have thought they had us pigeonholed at any given time. We were first a 'folk guitar' label. Even some of the folkies were offended; they said, 'This isn't folk music.' Okay, who said it was? Then we brought in Winston, and it was 'folk piano,' because it was on Windham Hill. As soon as somebody tells me what we are, I love to become something else. Right now, they're saying we're a jazz label, and Winston and I are planning an album of Gregorian chants."

Although their styles are fairly dissimilar, there is a lot of common ground among players such as Ackerman, de Grassi, Hedges and non-Windham Hill artists such as Pierre Bensusan, Steve Tibbetts, and others. For the most part, each came from a folk background. Ackerman's early influences were "Fahey and Basho, and to a lesser extent Renbourn, and to a far lesser extent Kottke," although he has all but abandoned the Faheyesque "double-thumbing" that typified early works such as "The Townshend Shuffle" [*It Takes A Year*] and "Seattle" [*Childhood And Memory*]. He

states: "I felt there was so much double-thumbing, and so much that was better, that this was not distinctively my style. I never felt any authorship of it."

Alex de Grassi is influenced more by Renbourn and Bert Jansch, slightly less by Fahey and Kottke. Bensusan's eclectic slant draws on folk styles from all over the world. Hedges represents a strange combination of rock energy, jazz training, and modern classical disciplines. Tibbetts is an unabashed child of rock and roll, with elements of Fahey, John McLaughlin, and Middle-Eastern music added as spice. All of these players have been affected to some degree by the acoustic jazz of Ralph Towner of the group Oregon, as well as the electric and acoustic playing of John Abercrombie and Pat Metheny, though Ackerman and de Grassi seldom improvise, while Tibbetts is constantly experimenting.

There are, of course, other guitarists who fall into the general category, including Preston Reed, with his Kottke-fueled 12-string excursions, Michael Gulezian, also a disciple of the Fahey/Kottke school, and Daniel Hecht, who recorded an album for Windham Hill in 1980. But the guitarists discussed here are bound together more by the fact that they are growing *out of* a tradition rather than starting a new one.

Ackerman will tell you that he is no great shakes as a technician—which is debatable. He is without doubt one of the most copied acoustic players. He reveals, "I get hundreds of tapes of people playing what they think I'll like, and inevitably they fail. I'm always amused that people will say, 'It's just like George Winston.' We've *got* George Winston. That's the worst tack in the world; bring me something new. I don't want 'Windham Hill,' or I wouldn't have recorded Mark Isham or [fusion group] Shadowfax. No one on the label is doing anything to be imitative or to be purposefully part of Windham Hill. This is what Alex de Grassi *feels*; this is the *core* of Liz Story. When somebody says, 'Ah, by going into an open tuning and writing a song that embodies many of the elements that are Windham Hill music, I can make a Windham Hill album,' if that isn't the core statement of this person as an artist, it probably won't translate as such."

The jazz tag that has been attached to Ackerman is one he has never been comfortable with. "I have never applied that term to myself, or the other guitarists on the label," Will stresses. "With small exception, we pay no homage to bebop or swing or blues. It's not in any sense an extension of a black urban experience. I think I'm exactly the same guitar player I ever was. I'm not a great player; I'm very limited in the range of tricks I have. If anything, I've become somewhat more polished, in terms of the very simple things one can do to manipulate a guitar—volume, tempo, dynamics. One enormous influence has been de Grassi. If you listen to 'Visiting' on my *Past Light* album, you can hear that. Alex' very linear, flowing, chord-over-chord style has been a major influence on what I'm doing right now—although obviously without the stretching of technical potential that Alex has. I'm not making any apologies for my style; it's just that it's very tightly defined as what I'm capable of. De Grassi is constantly pushing, and Hedges is reinventing, but I'm trying to get the most out of a narrow range of things."

Ackerman's method of composition lies in his use of unorthodox open tunings. Basically, he cranks the tuning machines until he arrives at a chord that instigates a melody. "Songs are discovered, not written," he explains. Will's self-taught tuning method is based entirely on intervallic relationships; in fact, he has no idea what note or chord values most of them have. "'Seattle' is a variation of open *D*," he details; "it reads 5 7 0 5 7, with no capo [translation: going high to low, the second string's 5th fret is the same pitch as the first string open; the third string's 7th fret equals the second string open; the fourth string open equals the third string open; etc.]. I've been working in a new tuning, which is 5 5 7 2 7 and capoed at the 5th fret. 'Bricklayer' is 5 5 5 5 5 all the way across, capoed at the 5th fret; 'Impending Death' is 7 1 7 4 8, capoed at the 2nd fret; and 'Processional' [all on *It Takes A Year*] is 1 4 3 7 5, capoed at the 5th fret."

As for recognizing any bond with other acoustic guitarists of his generation, Ackerman feels: "There's a kinship between Hedges, de Grassi, and myself that I wouldn't feel with, say, Kottke. Bensusan I'd include in our category. I think Fahey's best work is almost a wistful looking back, more than looking inward. It was always like John was painting somebody else's picture. I'm not knocking him; I love his music. But I feel that he was writing the book on a vanishing music, and what he studied as a musicologist, the old blues players, comes right through. It may just boil down to what's being communicated. I personally feel that the range of human emotions that are being attempted and communicated now are more subtle and intimate and personal. I don't think the range of human feeling that someone like Kottke was exploring is the same. His trademark was energy, and ours is more reflection. Hedges' is the most amazing thing in the world in that he can do both. He can be unbelievably dynamic, but at the same time tremendously reflective and emotionally evocative. I think the *purpose* of the music almost changed. It went from something demonstrative to something articulate." ☐

A Selected Will Ackerman Discography
Solo albums (on Windham Hill): *Turtle's Navel*, 1001; *It Takes A Year*, 1003; *Childhood And Memory*, 1006; *Passage*, 1014; *Past Light*, 1028; *Conferring With The Moon*, 1050.

DAROL ANGER AND
MIKE MARSHALL

By Elisa Welch Mulvaney

Frets, July 1987

Montreux Band members Darol Anger and Mike Marshall have blazed trails through some mighty wild musical territory to reach their current vantage point. As music students, teachers, instrument builders, collectors, sidemen, frontmen, composers, arrangers, new acoustic pioneers—and partners— they've played with a list of performers that reads like a *Who's Who* of acoustic string stylists: San Bush, Jerry Douglas, Bela Fleck, Stephane Grappelli, David Grisman, Mark O'Connor, Todd Phillips, and Tony Rice. To name a few.

Born in Seattle, Washington, Darol Anger studied classical violin as a youngster in New Jersey. When his family moved back west to California, he dabbled for a few years in rock guitar, then returned to the fiddle. In college at Santa Cruz, California, he developed a taste for bluegrass, eventually dropping his academic courses in favor of building instruments and playing tunes. In 1975, Darol met Todd Phillips, who had made mandolin bridges for David Grisman. One introduction led to another, informal jam turned into rehearsal, and in 1976 Darol became a founding member of the David Grisman Quintet.

Multi-instrumentalist Mike Marshall also spent his formative years on the east coast, first in Pennsylvania, then in Florida, where he received extensive training in music theory, ear-training, and bluegrass. At age 18, he had established his own school: Mike Marshall's Picking Parlor. Mike remembers, "When I heard that

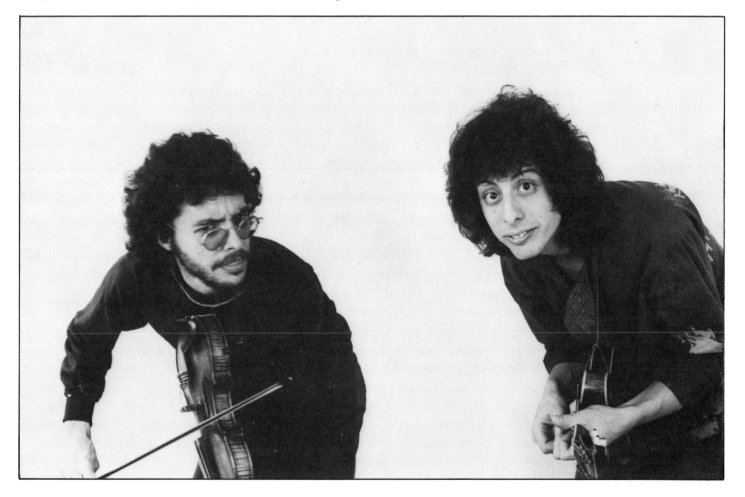

Darol Anger (left) and Mike Marshall.

9

first *David Grisman Quintet* album [1977], like everyone else I was floored, really inspired. I became a subscriber to David's magazine, *Mandolin World News*, and began corresponding with him. He extended an open invitation to visit."

On a trip west in 1978, Mike chanced to arrive when Grisman was having a bout with tendinitis. Grisman needed a stand-in mandolin player to dub some tracks for his score on the film *King Of The Gypsies*, and Mike got the job. Shortly thereafter, Mike joined the Quintet as second mandolinist.

Anger and Marshall established an almost instantaneous musical rapport. Darol remembers, "David gave us a lot of space to do mini-arrangements within the tunes. Also, he'd suggest either contrapuntal or harmonized things for us to do. And we were making up stuff standing next to each other onstage after a while. We had this affinity when we were playing melodically—we'd keep challenging each other.

"Mike was mostly playing mandolin in the Quintet while we had Tony Rice, and then Mark O'Connor, on guitar. He played some things on mandocello, and there were one or two pieces that had two guitar parts. But when Mark broke his arm [in 1981], suddenly Mike was the guitar player. That's one of the most amazing musical times I can remember: watching Mike switch over in the space of just a few days to become the band's guitarist."

When Mike moved in next door to Darol and pianist/fiddler Barbara Higbie, it seemed they were playing music all the time. "We always had duo and trio music projects going," says Mike, "and whenever we weren't touring with Grisman we were booking ourselves gigs at the folk clubs in town."

In 1979 Darol released a solo album, *Fiddlistics*, on which Mike and Barbara appeared as guests. Two years later Mike and Darol formed an experimental quartet—Saheeb—with Higbie and violinist David Balakrishnan. Balakrishnan's formal music studies preempted extensive touring, but Saheeb performed for enthusiastic audiences in the San Francisco bay area. In 1982, Darol and Barbara recorded a duet album, their first association with Windham Hill records: *Tideline*. Mike's first solo effort, *Gator Strut*, appeared on the Rounder label in 1984. That same year saw the release of another Rounder album: *The Duo*, with Marshall and Anger sharing the billing.

Amid these ongoing musical projects, Mike and Darol found themselves gradually outgrowing their backup roles in the Grisman band. "Actually, David

had more insight than we did," says Mike. "He could see that we needed other things musically, and was nice enough to—*gently*—say, 'Boys, it's time for a change here' [*laughs*]. And we were all too happy to oblige, because we had written all these tunes, and we wanted to get out there and play the music. We weren't saying 'Let's do a version of Grisman's music,' because we already had done that. It was more like, 'Let's see where *else* we can go.'"

Where they went was to Europe's prestigious Montreux Jazz Festival in the summer of 1984, where Darol and Barbara were to produce a sequel to *Tideline* for Windham Hill. The lineup included Mike, fellow Grisman alumnus Todd Phillips on bass, and Andy Narell on steel drums. Billed as the Darol Anger/Barbara Higbie Quintet, they recorded the highly acclaimed *Live At Montreux*.

The long association of Marshall, Anger, and Higbie, cast them into a more or less permanent musical entity; but both Narell and Phillips had busy agendas of their own. In 1986 an innovative bass player and Windham Hill artist named Michael Manring, sometime sideman for guitarist Michael Hedges, was invited to join the group. The Montreux Band was born.

Montreux's first release with its established lineup, *Sign Language*, showcases the ensemble's individual and collective talents. [*Ed. Note: See Darol's transcription of "Grant Wood," page 14.*] "We still have a lot of David Grisman's influence," offers Darol, "especially through Mike [Marshall], who generates quite a bit of the ongoing rhythm in both his mandolin and guitar playing. At the same time, Michael [Manring] does all that hammering, tapping, multi-finger technique on fretless electric bass, and that's putting us in a completely different area. We can get this tremendous driving rhythm even though everybody's playing *less.*"

Mike continues, "This is a learning experience, and it feels like a family of musicians. It helps that Barbara's in the band: She keeps it from being too much like a Texas fiddle contest."

No slouch as fiddler in her own right, Barbara Higbie admits, "that was my role in the early days. It seemed that in a lot of bands—particularly bluegrass bands—we saw an attitude where, if you didn't play *really fast,* you weren't considered good enough."

Michael Manring expands on the egalitarian approach to ensemble playing: "we've all played in bands where someone else was the boss, and in other bands where we've been the boss. So we're equally comfortable with either role—we can switch off any time." Higbie agrees, "We all have strong, independent, individual voices in this band; the secret is, we don't have any egomaniacs."

Darol is pleased with the direction the band is taking: "I think the basic progress that's been made is getting people to play different styles; getting different combinations of instruments; creating new ways of playing together in an ensemble."

Manring adds, "We don't limit improvisation to a solo instrument. Sometimes it will be a duo or trio thing; and when we're playing backup or rhythm behind it, we think of that as improvising, too."

Pinning a "style" on the Montreux Band's material is no mean feat. "Everybody has a different compositional style," says Darol, "though of course it's focused by the nature of the group. Mike might write a tune and he might have two or three melodies, two or three sets of changes, and two or three ideas of how it should all come together. We'll sit down and play it, and everybody has a lot of input. Eventually it falls together with everybody's various ideas. Barbara's kind of the same way, although she likes to throw in subtle stuff; sometimes it takes a while to uncover the tune."

What about his own approach? "I make sure that each tune I write is different from the one I wrote before," says Darol. "And there's at least one part that requires somebody to do something they've never done before."

Mike Marshall advocates a hands-on compositional technique: "I write like most string instrumentalists do, with the instrument in hand. Then I go through a series of yes-and-no questions, in terms of the band. For example, what will work for the piano? Or for a line that everybody's going to play?"

Marshall and Anger are pragmatic in their use of written music. Says Mike, "I tend to write out parts pretty much after the piece is composed—to make it easier to get it across to the other musicians." Darol adds, "I like the dynamic tension between highly arranged parts and parts that are completely improvised. So I might have a first page full of hundreds of little notes for everybody, and then the second page is just blank: 'Okay everybody, now figure out how to get from here to there.'"

In addition to performing new music composed by the members, the band has also adapted and expanded pieces that were originally conceived as solos or duets. Darol explains, "Even with the earlier material that we've adapted—like the violin and piano duets from *Tideline*, or music from *Chiaroscuro*—everyone has

been able to contribute so much, and so appropriately, that it seems like they were all conceived as Montreux Band tunes. Everybody's finding spots for themselves that complement each piece. I think that's a good argument for having four composers in a group. Everybody's really aware of not only their role, but everybody else's role. They're constantly adjusting to make sure that everybody is playing just the right thing.

"We all realize that each of us has to have outlets for ideas that don't necessarily apply to the whole band. For instance, Mike and Barbara and I play these triple-fiddle blowouts. We'll work out intricate introductions and endings and then just agree to go crazy in the middle, completely improvised. and Michael has incredibly inventive music for solo bass, so sometimes we'll just leave the stage and let him play."

Still, this doesn't detract from the band's ensemble atmosphere. On tunes that feature solo instruments, bandmembers gradually discover ways to play along. "We almost have to keep cutting away, keep pruning," allows Anger, "in order to make sure that everybody has enough space to express themselves. Everybody does solos in this group."

*   *   *   *

These days, Darol Anger divides his musical energies between the Montreux Band and the Turtle Island String Quartet. Darol is most enthusiastic about the Quartet because, he says, "It allows me to work with my old partner, David Balakrishnan. And we've found a couple of incredible players: Irene Sazer [violin and viola] and Mark Summer [cello]."

The quartet performs jazz and classical standards, utilizes written parts and improvised solos, and demands constant refining of Darol's "violin chops." That provided a suitable jumping-off point for a discussion of the "devil's box," and the techniques required to play it.

Do you consider yourself a fiddler, or a violinist?

I suppose I'd say that I'm a fiddler, because I like to improvise, and I don't have a strong classical background: I couldn't pass for a classical player.

Do you use traditional classical left-hand position?

I don't think it's quite as arched. Sometimes the position collapses and the heel of my hand comes up to the neck. But I always know when I'm doing that, because suddenly I can't reach the notes with my fourth finger any more. I have small hands, so it's important to try to keep a good hand position. I'm of the school: "If it feels right, go ahead and do it."

In a 1981 interview, you mentioned that you had to overcome a tight, nervous vibrato. How did you accomplish that?

I had to look at my whole way of playing and clean it up—totally revise it. Like people out in the real world, musicians get into bad habits that they're not aware of. The vibrato thing was really important for me. What I did to shake that was just not play *any* vibrato for about six months. You can hear that on the album *The David Grisman Quintet.* A lot of those notes I was consciously playing without any vibrato at all, because vibrato can be a way of avoiding coming to grips with intonation and proper hearing. On the next two albums, *Hot Dawg* and *Quintet '80,* you can hear the vibrato approach loosening up. I started playing a slow vibrato. For me, it took four or five years to get to the point of *using* the vibrato differently in each situation, as I do with the bow, for accent and effect.

How about your bow grip?

I use a classical bow-hold. Actually, when I was building instruments, I sliced the tip of my thumb off on a bandsaw. I had to use a Mark O'Connor/Byron Berline style bow-hold for about six months. And that felt right, I liked that style. You get a lot of leverage.

Is that a grip with the thumb down under the frog?

Kind of wrapped under the frog; it's a very relaxed hold. It's good for Texas-style fiddling, because you can get such a great legato. You can change bows [bowing direction] and nobody will even notice.

Do you use the whole bow, or do you favor one end in particular?

I tend to favor the upper half, but I use the lower part a lot too. Especially when I do rhythmic accents—the chunks and chops and slaps and whacks—I get way down by the frog. And, actually, my bow grip goes all to hell, my thumb bends back the other way. You know what it looks like? The way Vassar Clements holds the bow: It's kind of like you'd grab a baseball bat, or something. And I just go straight up and down on the strings to do the chunks.

How much rosin do you use?

Hardly any at all: I rosin the bow every week and a half or so. If I'm playing a lot, I'll rosin it more often. Or if I'm playing in difficult situations, I'll rosin the hell out of it, like if I'm having problems with the P.A., or if it's a loud group. It really depends on the situation, but I like it not-too-rosiny.

What kind of bow do you have?

It's a pretty good bow; I don't know who made it.

It's a little heavy at the tip, and it's very, very dense, springy wood, which I like. I don't have to tighten it too much. I like the feeling of the stick being really close to the hair. If it's too far away I feel like I'm playing out in space.

What kind of fiddle are you playing now?

I've got an instrument that is not only deep but very bright. It's about four years old now. It was made by Jay Ifshin from Berkeley [California]. From the very beginning, when I started on violin, I was dissatisfied with all the instruments I was playing. I changed violins about once a year. But this fiddle that Jay built for me—which is based on a Guarneri pattern—I've been really satisfied with. I haven't had any problems.

What kind of strings do you use?

Thomastik Dominants, which are those Perlon strings.

Do you use fine tuners?

Yeah. They're heavy, but it's really kind of a necessity. I have those little ones that sit in the [tailpiece] holes, and in trying to reduce the weight, I've drilled tiny little holes in the tuners themselves. They look like Swiss cheese; it's really funny. But I'm not completely happy unless I've tweaked something to within in inch of its life.

How often and how much do you practice?

It really varies. When I was first with Grisman I practiced more than I ever did in my life: three or four hours a day, every day, for about a year. And that's when my biggest advances came. In practicing, I like to get down to basics, and play really slow, long notes. I can't practice nearly as much as I'd like to, because I've been so busy trying to make a living and getting the Montreux Band happening. In fact, there was a period where I went for about six months without practicing ever—just picking the instrument up and going on-stage and playing it. There was definitely an effect on my playing which was *not* salutary. I'm getting back to practicing more, now. In fact, I've got a bunch of projects going that require it.

For instance?

There's the string quartet, of course. And I'm getting back into some serious bebop study; and also trying to adapt styles like [saxophonists] David Sanborn's and Hank Crawford's to the fiddle. Hardly anybody has been able to do that. It is very difficult, because there are such dynamic changes involved over the course of just a single note—vibrato and slides and things that don't immediately lend themselves to the violin.

What do you think listeners want from musicians?

I think people appreciate being able to recognize musicians by their playing. You feel like it's an old friend talking to you. It's like people writing letters saying "hello" to each other, and letting you know that they're okay, they're doing all right, or they're not doing that great, whatever. To me the central thing about music is communication.

*   *   *   *

Besides touring and recording with Darol Anger and the Montreux Band, Mike Marshall has more musical activities going on the side than most players attempt in their entire careers. Mike deftly juggles studio sessions, occasional teaching, and a new venture: the Modern Mandolin Quartet. "We wanted to call it the Mando Boys, but that was already taken" quips Mike. The Quartet features Mike and Dana Roth alternating on first and second mandolins; Paul Binkley on mandola; and John Imholz on mandocello.

What is your musical background?

I started out just a typical kid, taking guitar lessons. Then I studied with a multi-instrumentalist in Florida, Jim Hilligoss, and he opened up my ears to a lot of different things. To him, everything was hip—whether it was Italian mandolin music, Ventures guitar, the Beatles, or bluegrass. It was all music. Jim formed a group called the Sunshine Bluegrass Boys, from what he thought were his best bluegrass students, and he taught us how to play by ear and just have fun with it.

Why did you choose mandolin after starting out on guitar?

When the Sunshine Bluegrass Boys started going to festivals, that's when my mind really was blown about the mandolin and bluegrass.

Who were some of your early influences?

Jimmy Gaudreau and Doyle Lawson; and I learned a little bit from Bobby Osborne, and Jesse McReynolds. But I was even more interested in the newer guys, from Sam Bush forward. So that was what really blew my mind, that there was this traditional bluegrass instrument—and I really loved bluegrass—but look where some of these other cats were taking it.

Do you consider mandolin your main instrument?

I'll forever be a multi-instrumentalist. I love the guitar. I see myself as a utility infielder who covers what's needed in the band at the time: guitar, fiddle, mandocello, or whatever the tune calls for. But I'll always be really attached to the mandolin, because I feel the instrument deserves and needs people to take it further, in terms of trying to learn to play my instrument every day—that's an ongoing thing. There's forever a search for my own voice on the instrument.

Your own voice?

When you start out, you're inspired by other players. You try to imitate them. Every musician does this. I really learned a lot from Grisman, Tony Rice, Norman Blake, Sam Bush, and all the bluegrass heavyweights. Now it feels like I'm developing something of my own, something really personal.

Do you practice every day?

We've been touring so much, there isn't time every day for practicing. I play, of course. We'll show up at the soundcheck at 2, and we'll be playing off and on until 7. Then we'll take an hour off for dinner and go back and do the gig. So there's a lot of playing—always having the instrument in your hand—but I'd love to just get an hour to sit and kind of meditate with the instrument. Onstage you're putting it out, kind of throwing the chops away. It's good to get back and kind of regroup with your axe more personally.

Everybody has a certain thing that they're working on, whether it's "I'm going to learn this fiddle tune today," or "I'm going to figure out this rhythmic idea I hear in my head that my hands haven't quite gotten used to."

What are you working on?

I'm still working on tone. I think everybody should work on getting a good sound. That comes from thinking about the right hand: What do I have to do to project? Sometimes it's just playing a couple of notes, or one note, and understanding your instrument. Sometimes it's playing difficult things, or slowing them down and figuring out "Well, why doesn't this work here?"

Do you practice the parts you do in the band's arrangements?

There are things in the music we're doing now that are really difficult; so yes, I have to practice them. There are a couple of lines that aren't so hard to do slow, but getting them up to tempo is a real feat. That's fun—that's my "hot licks" work.

Can you recommend ways for musicians to get more adept on the mandolin fretboard, playing beyond first position?

First position falls so naturally on the instrument— its the first thing you learn. I think you have to learn about different keys. Learn to play a scale in first position, but without open strings. Then you have something that is moveable. Take a fiddle tune and re-finger it up the neck: Learn to play the same notes without any open strings. That way you're playing something you already know, mentally, and you'll know if you play a wrong note. Just take one problem on at a time. Don't try to learn a whole new tune up the neck; learn an old one in a new place.

What role do you play on mandolin in the Montreux Band?

I'm trying to develop a whole new style of playing rhythm mandolin in the music we're doing now. It came from Grisman and Sam Bush, but it also incorporates some of my own techniques and approaches from the guitar and mandocello. Michael [Manring] plays a lot of parts on the fretless bass—bass lines with interwoven melodic parts—and so my role changes. Sometimes I need to do octaves on the two high strings in some kind of rhythmic pattern, or sometimes crosspicking, to blend with him. My role is real dif-

ferent than it ever was in a bluegrass band or playing with Grisman. It feels like I'm doing something on the instrument that hasn't been done before.

What are you learning to do with instruments besides the mandolin?

I've been playing a lot of guitar these days. I'm trying to approach it less like jazz guitar, which uses a lot of closed-position chords. I've been trying to find new voicings for the instrument. Sometimes it's a muted, repetitive, single-note figure; sometimes it's open strums that should sound like cymbals crashing. I've been having a lot of fun with crosspicking, and finding out how the open strings relate to all the different keys you might be in.

For example?

If you're in the key of *E*, the open *E* and *B* strings work well. So I'll try fretting stuff on the lower strings while letting the *E* and *B* strings ring open. If you go to the key of *G*, the *D*, *G*, and *B* strings can be played open, so I'll work with fretting the other strings. [*Ed. Note: See Mike's transcription of "Dolphins," page 16.*]

What instruments do you own now?

Well I've got it pared down quite a bit. I've got the one 1924 Gibson Lloyd Loar F-5; that's pretty much the one I play all the time. I also have a 1920s Vega mandolin, and a John Monteleone mandocello. I have this 1966 Martin D-28 that I just love. I had gone through a few guitars, but something happened when I got this instrument. It had a bunch of tunes in there just waiting for me. I'm curious about trying harp guitar; talk about instantly getting a new musical voice! Just buy an instrument like that, lock yourself in a room for three years—and you'll have it. □

A Selected Darol Anger
and Mike Marshall Discography
Darol Anger, solo albums (on Kaleidescope, Box 0, El Cerrito, CA 94530): *Fiddlistics*, F-8. **With David Grisman:** *The David Grisman Quintet*, Kaleidescope, F-5. **With Matt Glaser and David Balakrishnan:** *Jazz Violin Celebration!*, Kaleidescope, F-22. **With Barbara Higbie:** *Tideline*, Windham Hill, C-1021. **Mike Marshall, solo:** *Gator Strut*, Rounder, 0208. **Mike and Darol:** *The Duo*, Rounder, 0168; *Chiaroscuro*, Windham Hill, 1043. **Mike and Darol with Montreux:** *Live At Montreux*, Windham Hill, 1036; *Sign Language*, Windham Hill, 1058.

"Grant Wood"

By Darol Anger

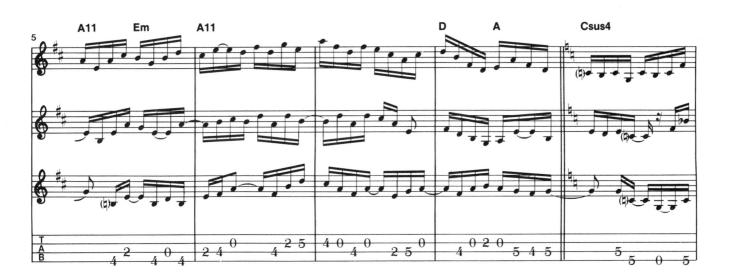

"Dolphins"

By Mike Marshall

Something I've been experimenting with is making standard guitar tuning sound like an open tuning—by utilizing the open strings and holding down every note as long as I can. The beginning of "Dolphins," from the *Chiaroscuro* album, illustrates some of these techniques.

In the first guitar part, hold the *D* and *F#* on the *G* and *B* strings while the melody notes *B, A,* and *G#* continue on the *E* string. You can use harmonics for the high *B* and *E* in measure 2. You could also play

the *E* on the open first string in measure 4, instead of stopping it on the *G* string.

In the third guitar part, the *B* drone in the bass is held with the thumb, and the 2nd and 3rd finger shift up and down on the middle strings, producing a slight portamento. To mute the *A* string on those chords, I bump it up against the 3rd finger on the adjacent string. Sixteenth-note up- and down-strokes can be added to give the tune a driving, subdivided feeling.

Notice how the open *E* string's role keeps changing in the third guitar part: In measure 6, it's the fifth of the *A* chord, and the suspended fourth of the *B* chord; then it's the root of the *E* chord in measure 7. It becomes the third of the *C#* minor in measure 8, and the added ninth of the *D* chord in measure 10.

—Mike Marshall

WILLIAM AURA

By Bob Doerschuk

Keyboard, October 1988

Twenty years ago William Aura was opening for the Amboy Dukes, the MC5, and Mitch Ryder, blowing his money, frying his brains, and otherwise leading a typical rock and roll life. Today he stirs mellow MIDIed brews in a studio overlooking the Pacific Ocean near Santa Barbara, mixing bird chirps and surf samples with synth textures on a series of popular cassettes. And unlike many who follow a similar aesthetic, Aura doesn't avoid the obvious label. He's a new ager, and proud of it.

If this sounds suspiciously like a born-again testimonial, there's good reason. Aura insists that getting involved with the new age movement helped him recover from the head-banging rigors of rock. Yet he also recognizes that there is more to modern new age than bliss and bean sprouts. It's a business now, he points out, with all the blessings and banes brought by success.

"In its roots, new age was about an almost egoless type of giving," he says. "But now the challenge is to keep the magic and the innocence that was the wellspring of this music, and apply it to making sure you get your royalty statement on time."

Few artists have kept these obligations as balanced as Aura. Though he has piloted his cassettes onto the playlists of more than 250 stations, he remains committed to the ideals that drew him into new age. "Everybody who has come to this style has had some sort of trouble in their lives, and that's true for me too," he explains. "When Eno came out with his *Music For Airports*, and Paul Horn with *Inside The Taj Mahal*, it was wonderful. But there were only five or six albums I really liked, so I started making tapes for myself and my friends in '79. By '84 I had sold about 50,000 units on my own over a five-or six-year period, so it was no big deal in numbers; I certainly wasn't in it for the money. Now, the acceptance of new age seems to be so massive that I'm blown away."

But what kind of new age music is it that audiences in the '80s have chosen to accept? Aura concedes that the style has changed significantly over the past few years. "New age music of the late '70s and early '80s was for relaxation, for self-healing, for guided imagery work, for driving your car, for having dinner, for making love to your favorite woman," he explains. "What's happened is that radio play has introduced pop influences, and the music has taken an uplifting turn. There's still a relaxation aspect, but some of the music is a little more aggressive. Some people think that this is a curse, but to me this new direction is wonderful. I did an album in '83 called *Paradise* [Higher Octave (8033 Sunset Blvd., Suite 41, Los Angeles, CA 90046), 7008], based on a Balinese scale, with steel drums, zither harp, bubbling brooks, a beautiful flute. It's still my best-selling tape. But to me, it's all candy. It's too sweet. The music has to go wider to survive. Now we can paint larger pictures. We can add a little bit of tension, so that you can feel resolution. It's a challenge to all new age artists, including me."

Though Aura was drawn into the new age largely because of its emphasis on healing and soothing, he has little sympathy for those in the movement who continue to think of the music only in these terms. At this point, Aura insists, it is imperative that old-guard followers take it more seriously, and stop impeding its evolution. "The New Age Music Network in L.A. consists of old new-agers," he says. "They haven't accepted that jazz can interact with new age. Instead, they come together every month and bitch about how impure the music is nowadays, and how they should change the world's view of what new age really is. They wanted me to be a part of this, but when I checked it out I saw that they were building a fence around themselves.

"The fact is that a new direction, a danceable, hummable, finger-snapping element, is coming in. Some people may feel that it's bastardized new age, but to me, if it takes you to the same place as the original music did, that's exciting. It doesn't matter how you get there, as long as you enjoy the journey."

Toward that end, Aura is adapting what he learned from his first new age projects to a more modern tempo. "My next album, which will be out in January, is

new age dance music," he says. "Back in '82 we did some biofeedback tests. A couple of my albums are at 60 beats per minute, so we attached electrodes to people and watched how their bodies reacted. Within five minutes, their hearts would pace with the beat. It worked like a charm every time. That taught me that a few of the things I'd been doing intuitively had some scientific merit. So we started looking at polyrhythms. I'd put a rhythmic zither strum in the right ear of a person hooked up to biofeedback gear, and they'd start pacing to that strum. When we introduced an arhythmic strum in the left ear, and their consciousness attempted to follow both, they lapsed into a hypnotic state in about two minutes. We had discovered something that people knew eons ago—that polyrhythms can be used for hypnotic induction, for altered states of consciousness, even for soul travelling. Why not take this information and use it for sequenced polyrhythms in dance music?"

Why not go even further, and borrow directly from jazz or rock? "I was really thinking about that in '84 and '85," Aura remembers. "When I released *Fantasy* [Higher Octave, 7006], that was the first one of my albums to get some jazz activity by virtue of the fact that it featured what I called a 'pop indicator'—a saxo-

phone. We found that if you take a new age piece and add one indicator—by dropping in a sax break, for example—by God, it's jazz! Change that to a synthesizer patch, and it's not jazz! I was feeling other limitations in '84 and '85 too. I began wondering how many times I could do something with that damn Balinese scale. To me, a record is a statement of time and place. Once I've made that statement, I don't want to make it again the following year. So now I take my cue from Andreas Vollenweider, who runs you through quite a few emotions in his music. I'm feeling less limited than ever."

Greater technical resources have also helped broaden Aura's range. A former metal guitarist, he now specializes in synths, samples, and sequences, relying most often on his Roland D-50, Akai S900, Ensoniq Mirage and ESQ-1, and Macintosh with Opcode software. "Opcode is much more new age than Performer," Aura laughs. "Performer seems best for people who start at the beginning of a song and play all the way through. Most new agers aren't necessarily that proficient. Certainly, I'm no virtuoso. So we tend to focus on patterns instead. And it's possible to use all this gear intuitively. They say that MIDI is new, but come on! From what some of these psychics have said about Atlantis, we've had this technology before." □

PETER BARDENS

By Bob Doerschuk

Keyboard, October 1988

Nearly fifteen years ago, while most progressive rock bands were still mutating Keith Emerson licks, Camel was stretching the style's boundaries. In 1975, this intelligent and ambitious quartet was dabbling in minimalism, with Peter Bardens bravely arpeggiating dense textures on his monophonic Minimoog and ARP Odyssey. And though they were faithful to the progressive gospel, the band also cast occasional glances toward a more contemplative style. They even recruited Brian Eno for one cut, "Elke," from *Rain Dances,* whose pastoral stillness anticipated Eno's landmark *Music For Airports* by a couple of years.

Fast-fowarding to the mid-'80s, we catch Bardens on his own. His solo albums—most recently *Seen One Earth* [Cinema (dist. by Capitol), 12555] from 1987, and this year's *Speed Of Light* [Cinema, 48967]—reflect the temper of different times. The colors are richer, thanks to Bardens' fine ear for orchestration, which allows him to sew synths from years past and the latest gear into a seamless, timeless fabric. Free from the fixation with structural complexity that helped antiquate prog rock, he has developed a style that incorporates silence, simplicity, consonant themes, and rhythms that unobtrusively pace milky electronic lines, then perhaps dissolve into static white noise washes.

And yet . . .

"This is not new age music," Bardens growls. "It's a drag that everything has to be pigeonholed and labeled. I mean, I like to feel that what I'm doing is not a cult thing. I want it to communicate, to cross over so that people who are into Iron Maiden or the Beastie Boys can get something out of it too."

Okay. Let the record show that Pete Bardens disavows any connection with new age music. His credentials are pure rock and roll, embracing a number of groups in England's feverish R&B scene of the '60s, Van Morrison, Colin Blunstone, and Captain Sensible of the Damned, as well as Camel. "You can't shake off 20 years of musical experience," he insists. "And I don't want to. What I'm doing now is very much an extension of that. I

tend to approach what I do from the standpoint of having played in bands. *Speed Of Light* is essentially rock music that sounds really good when played by at least four or five guys. It has to be played live at a reasonable volume onstage."

For that reason, Bardens sees important differences between his approach and the path followed by new age artists in putting solo projects together. "I'm not Patrick O'Hearn, Mark Isham, or Kitaro," he declares. "I'm not trying to do keyboard extravaganzas on my albums. Instead, I'm trying to project that group sound by using recognizable sounds—violins, saxes, bass guitars, and so on."

Of course, he gets most of these sounds on keyboard instruments of one type or another. Though buttressed by guest musicians, Bardens' solo albums are mainly his own handiwork. "I used a broad spectrum of synthesizers on *Speed Of Light,*" he reports. "Everything from Minimoog to a Kurzweil. There's a Fairlight, and a little bit of PPG. I used a D-50 for the first time; it's good for transparent sounds that don't cloud everything up. There's even a Hammond B-3, toward the end of 'Gold.' I just like having fun with sounds, whether they're old or new. I tried to combine them all within the context of a band, so that you've got things that sound like basses, and things that sound like guitar. Some of the really wired, heavy fuzz guitar is from the [E-mu] Emulator II. When I played those lines, I really tried to imagine that I was actually playing guitar. Same thing with the sax lines, which also came from the Emulator; I'd imagine myself like [saxophonist] Grover Washington, in a white suit, a fedora, and shades."

And yet . . .

Along with the hard-edged beat and vocals that animate some cuts on *Speed Of Light,* there are softer moments—the celestial choir and Winston-like piano figure on "Afterthought," the open voicings and breathy textures on "Westward Ho!"—which seem to acknowledge a shift in public taste away from razor-slash rock toward something more contemplative. Even the throbbing percussion on "Heartland" wouldn't sound out of place on today's adult contemporary charts. Certainly *Seen One Earth* is awash with dreamy timbres, flowing consonant melodies, and other elements that new age artists have employed before. You can even hear a few bird-like chirps in "Seascape."

"*Seen One Earth* was a concept album," Bardens patiently explains. "Okay, it was on the Cinema label, but it wasn't directed at a new age audience. Far from it. Actually, I think it went for the jugular. I think it really crystallized my outlook, which is essentially from the rock standpoint rather then from anything else. Would you not agree with that?"

Absolutely. Still, the lesson posed by Bardens' work is that artists of proven ability in one or another style can be affected by the massive impact being wrought by new age and adult contemporary music. Perhaps we might detect something else here too—an understandable reluctance to be categorized, particularly in a style whose philosophical foundations hold little appeal for Bardens. Even now, 14 years after *Music For Zen Meditation*, this inextricable association of philosophy and style remains the albatross around the neck of new age music.

"In a lot of cases, new age music seems to have been designed to provide an inoffensive and innocuous kind of background," he says. "And I, as a musician, have never wanted to make musical wallpaper. Obviously, some of the things I've recorded have a sort of calming effect, but they're also designed to wake you up and make you sing. I do like some new age music. For example, I like Kitaro a lot. His music has a warmth and dynamic element that I can relate to, even though he's classified as new age. But I don't see that as taking over from essential, solid, progressive rock music."

As we went to press, Pete Bardens, progressive rock survivor and AOR virtuoso, was looking into the possibility of taking *Speed Of Light* on the road. There was talk of opening an international tour in England or Germany, featuring Bardens backed by a hard-hitting, no-bones-about-it, rock band. "I don't want to go back to the old days of endless improvisation," he says. "In the Camel days that was expected. Doing a 20-minute organ solo, followed by a 25-minute guitar solo, was a part of the music. That was one of the things that killed off progressive rock to a large extent. I'm not trying to

prove anything anymore. I'm just trying to create straight-ahead, direct, no-bullshit music."

And yet . . .

"Yes," he wearily acknowledges, "that textural spacey element has always been a part of my music. But not to the exclusion of the more foot-tapping or even head-banging side. I don't want to isolate one aspect of music and dwell on that. I'd rather incorporate that into the context of the whole thing. Do you know what I'm trying to say?"

Message received. Loud (and soft) and clear. □

PIERRE BENSUSAN

By Rick Gartner

Frets, May 1987

When he feels restless, he just finds a new challenge. Winning the Montreux Jazz Festival's 1979 Grand Prix du Disque with his first LP (*Pres de Paris*) was a good start for a 17-year-old musician. Over the next few years French finger-style guitarist Pierre Bensusan has composed and recorded the material for three more albums, with an ambitious schedule of international concert tours. Now he's looking beyond the usual recording and touring regimen, and looking beyond the six strings of the standard acoustic guitar.

Bensusan's most recent project—a collection of his solo guitar pieces—is typical of his imaginative work. It is a hardbound volume complete with music (from all four Bensusan LPs), with philosophy, and impressionistic art. This holistic collection, the *Pierre Bensusan Guitar Book*, (dist. by International Music Network, Box 411, Mill Valley, CA, 94941), is being translated into several languages, and the English version should be available soon. This impressive anthology is entirely self-produced, and has been several years in the making.

Bensusan isn't afraid to be different, from his extensive use of electronic effects to his exclusive use of "Dadgad" tuning. He pursues whatever interests him, and his music—a unique blend of Western and Eastern elements—is always interesting. In the following interview, Pierre discusses his new directions and his new instruments.

* * * *

*M*uch of your energy for the last couple of years has been devoted to your book. It's something quite different than one might expect.

Yes, it has been a giant work. You know, I felt honored that many people expressed to me that they wanted to learn my tunes. So I wanted to make this possible, but I also wanted this book to be something more—a work of art in itself. So we spent much time and energy in this production, and it is very gratifying to see the result of all this effort.

So this has become much more than just a songbook to you?

Much more. I was experiencing a problem that many touring musicians go through, feeling like I was losing some control of my artistic career—that it was beginning to control me. I felt that there are many ways to give the people a souvenir of my art; something other than just giving concerts and making records. By doing the book, I can also create another base of income, so that I can stay home more, and really concentrate on composing new music. I'm hoping it's possible to have a life where I don't have to go on the road every year.

Was the touring starting to drain too much of your energy?

When you spend so many weeks on the road, the concerts lose something of the special feeling. It should be an event, something where you give 100 percent of yourself. The concert is the instant of creation for your art. Sometimes I would be so tired that I found myself onstage pretending my art. So when I thought of ways to balance out my life, I began thinking of other mediums. I want to look *forward* to my concerts—not see them as something I *must* do in order to make money. Hopefully this book will be the first of many steps I can take to adapt my life so that I can continue with my art, and be happy.

Has this discipline of writing out your music started to give you insights into your own creative process, and produce new ideas for compositions?

Yes. I am beginning to do more analysis of music—my music, the music of others. Now every day I do some reading of music. I find that this is giving me the ability to more easily bring out what I hear inside my head, as I gain more facility at writing the music. So already there are many benefits before making money. I am beginning to see music as a story that you tell, but with a very precise structure to it, and organization that goes with the feelings you express.

Speaking of precision, you show both your right- and left-hand fingerings in great detail in your book. Do you advocate that kind of systematic approach?

Well, I think you really need to be systematic, especially in the faster or more difficult passages. But just as I don't necessarily feel that my fingerings are the best ones for all players I think we all need to be open to making refinements in fingering as we learn a piece. And I think we should be open to changes even on pieces we feel we've mastered. Anything that makes the music come more to life. You need to be somewhat settled sooner or later, so that you can have the notes automatic, and then you can work on becoming more expressive within that structure. If you're always having to think of how you're going to finger a piece, you can't work for the colors and the subtleties.

What about the music itself? Do you feel free to make changes when you learn someone else's music?

First, I think we should learn the music the way a composer intended it. But I don't think we should feel trapped when we reach the point of understanding the composer's intention. At that point we can really concentrate on what we might like to hear. Then I think you can make changes by adding some syncopations, or exercise some freedom in the bass. Everything is

open to question, but we must be careful not to use this as a license to avoid the understanding process of learning the composer's original intention.

Are you beginning to think of bringing in instruments other than the guitar for your recordings?

Very much. I now am seeing and thinking of orchestration as a way to be a better storyteller in music. It is new for me, but I know it has already changed my way of thinking about music, to go beyond the guitar.

It sounds like you may be starting to look toward leading a band sometime soon.

Always before, playing solo has felt very natural, and one should do what feels natural. But yes, now that I am looking toward orchestrations I will want to share the stage with other musicians. I have been feeling frustrated recently as a solo player, not being able to really play what I hear inside. Sometimes I hear everything *but* the guitar, all the other instruments playing an arrangement. In fact, I think my next American tour won't be a solo tour. You know, there is only so much you can do as a soloist, even with all the effects, programs and other resources we now have. You need the energy of other musicians; the ideas of other players. This I find very exciting to think about.

Even with your own instrument, you are looking at some major changes. Tell us about the new guitars you are having built for you.

First, there is going to be a 10-string guitar, one that George Lowden is making for me. There will be the normal six strings, which will be steel. We will probably use classical strings for the other four strings, which will all be bass strings.

Why are you going to use classical strings for the extra basses?

So we don't have to make the instrument too heavy; we want to keep the bracing light.

Will the four bass strings be over the fretboard, like those on 10-string classical guitars?

Yes. Right now I am thinking that I will tune the lowest string to *D*, an octave below the *D* on my 6-string guitar—which as you know I always tune *D A D G A D*. Then after the lowest bass *D* I probably will tune the other three extra bass strings *F A C*.

Did you say that you will indeed tune the next six strings to D A D G A D, *exactly as you do on your 6-string guitar?*

That is what I am thinking of now. I want to say that the purpose of this new guitar is not to achieve new summits of technique, or put on a visual display. It is for one purpose: to be able to play those low bass notes that I hear in my mind, but cannot play on the guitar I now have. Sometimes just the addition of one extra bass note can add something that is very beautiful and deep.

But it's going to take some getting used to. Will you abandon your 6-string, at least for a while?

That is how it will have to be, in all probability. And my wish is to become so comfortable and natural with this new guitar that I won't think of it as something different, just something more. My inspiration for this is [Brazilian guitarist] Egberto Gismonti.

Recently, you've been moving much more toward an acoustic-electric sound with various effects, especially onstage. Is all of this work with new instruments and acoustic-electrics a sign that the acoustic 6-string has lost favor with you?

I still love the sound of the acoustic 6-string, but I like to add today's technology. Actually I feel myself moving back toward the acoustic sound lately, because I think sometimes it is too easy to punch in reverb, delays, and chorus. I want to achieve a better balance between these new doors and new colors and the natural sound of the pure acoustic guitar. Then there

are times when I would like people to forget that I am a guitarist, and to be taken with just the music. The effects are one way to change the sound so that what the people hear is something very different than what they expect to hear.

So you're open to anything. That comes across in your compositions. You go from something that sounds like an Irish reel into a Middle-Eastern mode without stopping to breathe. Then when you do breathe you start scat singing in a jazz style. How do you see the influences in your music?

I try not to think of this. I just create the sounds somewhere within all that which I have experienced. I make it all from my personal synthesis. If I think about it, I might get trapped by too much analysis. It is a world music, and this is a trend I see everywhere I travel. With all the communications from culture to culture, this is inevitable. This is not an age of limitations, as it was for Bach. Of course, I grew up in Algeria, and so I lived around the musics of North Africa, closer to the Arabic influences that can be found in all music, if you look deep enough.

So you feel that musicians should look beyond their own cultural borders?

I feel that there should be no borders. Sometimes I feel that guitarists think too much of themselves, of their guitars, and tend to make these borders. So they cannot expand. I feel that is especially true here in America. Often I feel that America is like an enormous cultural island. They stay in the borders of mode and sound that have been created here. It can make their music too simplistic.

What do you suggest for those players who don't get a chance to travel?

To listen to the musics of South America, of India, of Africa—all the music of the world. Be curious about what is going on all over the world. As you turn away from what is familiar to your experience you will be able to go beyond the borders of your own experience. Without effort, your music will expand. Then with some work you will find the new techniques to express your feelings. □

A Selected Pierre Bensusan Discography
Solo albums (on Rounder, 1 Camp St., Cambridge, MA 02140): *Pres de Paris*, 3023; *Pierre Bensusan 2*, 3037; *Musiques*, 3038; *Solilai*, 3068.

ALEX de GRASSI

By Dan Forte and Jas Obrecht

Like his cousin Will Ackerman, Alex de Grassi used to think of himself as a carpenter who played guitar on the side—in fact, he used to work under Ackerman at what was then called Windham Hill Builders. After Will recorded two solo guitar albums, he decided to release an anthology of fingerstyle guitarists, and put de Grassi in a studio. The result was not a sample LP but Alex de Grassi's 1798 debut solo release, *Turning: Turning Back*. "It took me forever to record the first album—over a period of a year," he relates. "I realized when I got in there that I wasn't really prepared, and I didn't know what it took to get recording-quality takes. On the next record, *Slow Circle*, we went in and did it in 15 hours over three-and-a-half days. By that time, I'd been out playing concerts a lot more, and I'd learned the hard way—from doing *Turning: Turning Back*. *Clockwork* [*his third effort*] came at a time when I wanted to do something other than just the solo thing. The tunes I'd written clearly weren't solo guitar tunes. I enjoyed doing it, and I still like the music, but it was my first time in the role of producer and, in effect, arranger, so I was under a lot of pressure. Looking back, I think I made some mistakes that I'd change if I were doing it again."

Those three albums showed de Grassi to be one of the leading figures of the new school of steel-string guitarists. British folk influences such as Bert Jansch and John Renbourn intermingled with sensibilities borrowed from modern jazz greats Ralph Towner and John Abercrombie in de Grassi's self-described "twisted" compositions. At the time of its release, 1981's *Clockwork* was easily the most unusual item in the Windham Hill catalog, with its blend of solo and ensemble pieces and mixture of electric and acoustic instruments—played by Missing Persons bassist Patrick O'Hearn, violinist Darol Anger, mandolinist Mike Marshall, saxophonist Chuck Greenberg, pianist Scott Cossu, and others.

Southern Exposure marked a return to solo acoustic

guitar, and is possibly de Grassi's most realized work as a composer and guitarist. The songs are less stream-of-consciousness, more melodic; the playing is cleaner in execution and clearer in tone. Overall, the album portrays Alex de Grassi as a mature artist who continues to evolve.

For nearly a decade, Alex de Grassi was exclusively associated with Windham Hill Records. His 1987

Guitar Player, February 1985 and June 1987

release, *Altiplano*, signals a major change in the guitarist's musical direction. The project features an eclectic array of instrumentalists—fretless bassist Mark Egan, tabla master Zakir Hussain, and violinist Jamii Szmadzinski amoung them—and often couches the guitar in a supporting role. While a couple of tracks are reminiscent of his earlier work, de Grassi ventures into jazz, Brazilian, Middle Eastern, and pop flavors. He recorded *Altiplano* with steel-strings crafted by luthiers George Lowden and Erwin Somogyi, a John Mello classical guitar, and an Ibanez guitar synth.

* * * *

The tunes on your first two albums seemed to be more mood pieces, whereas Southern Exposure *is made up of definite songs.*

Well, I've been playing guitar since I was 13, but I never really committed myself to being a musician. When I went to record *Turning: Turning Back* and *Slow Circle*, even though I was more prepared the second time, I didn't write the pieces out at all, I didn't think about the chords I was playing, it was all open tunings. That whole approach to playing guitar on those two albums is very idiomatic—what I mean by that is it's just picking. I think that has a fascination for guitar players perhaps because it's very guitar-oriented music. It's not something that would adapt well to other instruments. But with *Southern Exposure,* the music started a little more in the head maybe, and the process of writing music was a little more conscious. I even had to sit down at the piano and work out part of the title tune. That album shows me more as a composer, rather than someone who just sits down and plays stream-of-consciousness.

Were the ensemble pieces on Clockwork *written with a structure as defined as your solo compositions?*

Some of them are improvised to an extent, some aren't. "Thirty-six" [recorded with an ensemble on *Clockwork*] I'd written initially as a solo piece, and I re-recorded it on solo guitar on *Southern Exposure.* "Two-Color Dream" is structured like a jazz tune, with a head, a bridge, and a solo section, where the soprano sax blows over that with me being part of the rhythm section. "Clockwork" was very structured, with a lot of changes in meter, and I wrote out the melody for the Lyricon [woodwind synthesizer controller].

Do you read music?

I'm getting better. I've been sight-reading a lot of classical and Brazilian things.

Are you playing those pieces in standard tuning?

Yes. Most of the songs on *Clockwork* were in standard tuning, too.

The improvising on Clockwork *was mostly done by the other instruments.*

That's true. I'm getting into improvising more now. I wrote a lot of the pieces for *Clockwork* with specific instruments in mind. I used the guitar more as a compositional tool. I've written some new pieces I've been playing with Darol Anger and [pianist] Barbara Higbie where I solo, too.

Will Ackerman's collaborations with other instrumentalists seem much less structured—sometimes just a chord pattern on guitar with a solo played by another instrument.

I had the melodies all written out, and the players read what I'd written. Will lets the players kind of make the melodies up themselves. I don't think Will reads or writes music—which is fine—and he doesn't necessarily have a melody that he's humming when he comes into the studio. It's more like, "Here's what I'm playing; play something over it." Then if he's trying to push it in a certain direction, he talks about it in more metaphysical terms: "Get more water into it." He tries to work with the image more, which is good. It's important to be true to the feeling of the music. One of the things I've concluded is that when writing for a group, I really try to simplify and strip things down to get the feeling.

You work with a few set tunings, rather than Ackerman's method of turning the keys until a tuning falls into place and then composing a song that's a product of that tuning.

The song is, in a way, a product of the tuning. I guess the question is the old chicken and the egg—which came first, the tuning or the musical idea? On the first two albums, the tuning really determines a lot about how the music is. By the time of *Southern Exposure,* where I'm using both open and standard tuning equally, the musical idea dictates the tuning more. It was more like, "If I'm going to do this, I'm going to have to tune these strings down," whereas before it was, "Hey, that's a neat-sounding chord; let me see what I can get out of that."

Are there songs on Southern Exposure *that you could not have played at the time of* Turning: Turning Back*—either because of their complex structures or the degree of technique required?*

I don't think so. "Overland" is a very difficult piece to play, but what makes it hard are the positions you must hold with the left hand, and the stress factor. Early reviewers of my music always talked about the right hand, but for me, the fast picking in "Overland" isn't particularly hard. When I finally recorded it, I had to use light-gauge strings, instead of medium-gauge, because I couldn't make it through the whole song without getting really fatigued. When I first went out to perform these new pieces, I was having a little problem with muscle tension in my hands, so I haven't played "Overland" in concert, but I intend to work it up. It's in standard tuning with the bass tuned down to *D*, and I tried to figure out how to play it in an open tuning so I could get around the long stretches with the left hand, but I couldn't. So there's something idiomatic about a tuning that gives it a certain quality—the sound of open strings versus fretted strings, different resonances. But the pieces I find hardest to play are a couple on *Turning: Turning Back*—in particular "Blood And Jasmine," which is probably the most technically difficult piece I've ever written.

Before you got the Somogyi you're using now, what kind of acoustic did you play?

A blonde maple Guild F-50. I use medium-gauge strings and pick with a thumbpick and my fingernails. If you play a dreadnought-size guitar or bigger, you have to use heavier strings to get any volume. For fingerstyle playing, I always thought the smaller guitars like the 0-bodied Martins sounded better with light gauge strings. I bought a really nice classical from a builder named John Mello in Berkeley [California]. It's not quite as deep a body, and it's very light construction, so it's a little like a flamenco guitar. It's somewhere between the sweetness of a classical and the brightness of a flamenco. I also have a Ron Ho 12-string. Ervin Somogyi first approached me after a concert and let me play one of his guitars. Then I went to his shop and played the one I have now, which wasn't even finished yet—the neck was still rough-hewn—but I loved it. So he shaved the neck down to the depth I like. It was his idea to have the fingerboard wider than a traditional steel-string's, which I really like.

Somewhere between your first and fourth albums did you pick up new influences that affected your writing and playing?

Yes. I started getting into a lot of South American music, which shows up a little on the second side of *Clockwork*. A couple of the songs on *Southern Exposure*, like "Blue And White," use some of those types of chords. There's so much happening in South American

music; from a guitar standpoint, there always has been—people like Baden Powell, Luis Bonfa, and Antonio Carlos Jobim.

Were the majority of your early guitar influences folk players?

Pretty much. I've always felt there's been kind of a lag between me as a performer and the type of music I've been influenced by. I think most people would hear *Turning: Turning Back* as a folk album, with maybe a little bit of classical feeling, too. Certainly my early influences were players like John Renbourn and Bert Jansch. When I first got a nylon-string guitar, I played folk tunes and Beatle songs. Then I got a steel-string, and got a little bit into people like Mississippi John Hurt. But when I first got hold of Bert Jansch's album *Lucky 13*, I said, "Man, I've got to learn those pieces." So I used the needle-drop technique and finally pulled four or five tunes off that record. That really got me fired up about playing solo steel-string guitar. And even ten years later, when I recorded my first album, he was still a strong influence, along with John Renbourn and Davey Graham. "Inverness" on *Slow Circle* has that sort of feeling, too.

At that point, critics started comparing you to Ralph Towner and calling your music jazz.

Like I said, there's always been a lag between what I was recording and what I was listening to. *Turning: Turning Back* was recorded in 1978, and most of the pieces were written from '74 to '77—and "Alpine Medley," which is more Kottke-inspired, even earlier. But I'd been listening to all the ECM records for a while. I'd been listening to Keith Jarrett since 1964—and Charles Lloyd's *Forest Flower* [Atco, 1473]. The first thing I wrote that reminded me at all of Ralph Towner was "Klamath" on *Slow Circle*.

What's your feeling about yourself and the artists on Windham Hill being classified as jazz?

I don't think of myself as a jazz musician, even though some tunes, like "Street Waltz" [*Southern Exposure*], are jazz-flavored. I'm incorporating the jazz influence more into what I'm doing. But if you talk to somebody like [trumpeter] Wynton Marsalis, he's not going to call us jazz, and he's right, from his viewpoint. We don't go out there and play changes and blow over the top. I think over a period of time, the body of the music changes, and everybody's picking up different influences. For practical reasons, people want to draw lines—black, pop, jazz, country, classical, folk. But on the other hand, I don't get invited to folk festivals. People don't think of me as folk music, because there's nothing traditional or folk-rooted about me—although there's a little bit of that British Isles influence. But do you call somebody like Egberto Gismonti jazz? He's not out there blowing over changes either.

How do you feel about being associated with the so-called Windham Hill family and new age music?

First of all, if I put myself in the shoes of the record-buying or concert-going public, I remember the first ECM album I bought by Keith Jarrett. Then I realized that there were other ECM records, and at some point I thought, this is a pretty hip label, and I would start to buy ECM albums blind. I think that's happened naturally with whoever the audience is for Windham Hill, and I think Will has encouraged that. There are times when I don't always like that. On the one hand, I have to say it's good for me in terms of promotion and selling more records—no doubt about it. On the other hand, I've had a slight negative feeling on some occasions from the Windham Hill Live shows, because it turns into a kind of talent show, in a way. Everybody gets to play for 15 minutes, and the audience is supposed to like everything, because, hey, it's Windham Hill. But there is diversity. Not everybody who comes to see one of the artists is going to want to hear all the others—although there's a good chance.

What inspired your new direction displayed in Altiplano?

It's been about three years since I made a record, and in addition to traveling and playing, I took some time off to learn a lot of new things. I spent some time playing the classical guitar and getting some basic keyboard skills so that I can write and orchestrate better. I got into playing jazz tunes—sight-reading and improvising—and did a few duo gigs with Bruce Forman, who's pretty mainstream. I looked for outlets that forced me to learn new tunes and get my chops together. Although I'm still pretty much of a novice, I began studying about synthesizers. My 1980 *Clockwork* album was a change for me, too. This time I'm trying to stretch out and be more of a composer and an arranger. I want to feature the guitar, but not necessarily have it dominate each piece. So I hope the album reflects some musical growth and expansion into completely new areas.

Where on Altiplano *do you play guitar synth?*

I used an Ibanez MC1 for the melody voice in "Fat Boy." Originally I wanted to get more of a distinctly guitar synth sound, but due to my limited technical ability at this point [*laughs*], I couldn't get all the pitch-bends happening just the way I wanted. I had the

Ibanez MIDI'd into a Roland synth and an Ensoniq ESQ1 [synthesizer with built-in sequencer]. Although it's done on guitar synth, that melody probably could have been played with the same effect on a keyboard.

The album merges many diverse styles.

Yes. The middle section of "Fat Boy" has an acoustic guitar break that uses a tuning I've used a lot in solo guitar playing—$E\,B\,E\,F\sharp\,B\,E$, starting with the low string. But since I wrote this tune in $E\flat$ on the piano, I tune everything down a half-step; conceptually, though, it's the same tuning. The solo guitar piece "McCormick" is in $D\,A\,D\,G\,C\,F$, the same tuning I used for "Heavy Feet" on *Southern Exposure*. The song is in the key of F, so the tonic is derived from the top string, which is frequently used open as a drone. "Digital Interlude," which is a duet with Mark Egan, is in $D\,A\,D$ $G\,C\,E$. That song fluctuates through a couple of different keys—it has an A minor and a D modal feeling to it.

Have you separated yourself from the Windham Hill label?

I have in terms of my future recording plans. I signed a "two-plus-two" contract with RCA/Novus, meaning that I'll definitely be doing a second album, and if everyone's satisfied, I'll do two more. I like to think that I'm still on reasonably good terms with Windham Hill, and recording for them was obviously very good for my career. But psychologically it was a good time for me to step away from the label. I wanted to stretch into directions that weren't necessarily the kind of thing that they would get behind 100 percent. And, frankly, I wanted to get away from the label's image. Suddenly it had somehow become more powerful, meaningful, and in a way more generic. It gave me a sense that I was part of a generic new age phenomenon that would go on with or without me. The Windham Hill image was so overwhelmingly strong that it didn't allow me to create my own career and artistic image in the way that I'd want to do it. It was a tough decision. □

A Selected Alex de Grassi Discography
Solo albums: *Altiplano*, RCA/Novus, 3016-4-N; (on Windham Hill): *Turning, Turning Back*, 1004; *Slow Circle*, 1009; *Clockwork*, 1018; *Southern Exposure*, 1030.
With others (on Windham Hill): *Windham Hill Sampler '82*, 1024; *Windham Hill Sampler '84*, 1035.

MARK EGAN

By Tom Mulhern

Sitting in a New York studio with his double-neck bass, Mark Egan is strategically positioned between several huge electric fans, letting one set of his instrument's strings sustain as the air rushes past. He isn't cooling the instrument after a hot solo; he's simulating the sound of the breeze surging through a lush Hawaiian valley for a cut on his first solo album, *Mosaic.* A month later, he's in Paris laying down fretless lines with Duran Duran's keyboardist Nick Rhodes and vocalist Simon Le Bon. That project's followed by soundtracks for a

windsurfing movie called *Blown Away* and the film version of *A Chorus Line.*

At 34, Mark Egan is a cofounder of Elements, a sonically rich ensemble that experiments as much with sound as it does with musical forms. (Elements, with cofounder/drummer Danny Gottlieb, also features saxophonist Bill Evans and keyboardist Clifford Carter; both Evans and Gottlieb also work with John McLaughlin and others.) Mark's main thrust for the past three years, Elements has recorded a pair of albums, *Elements* and *Forward Motion,* and toured and

Guitar Player, September 1985

enrolled in private lessons from fifth grade through high school. Although playing only trumpet at the time, Mark identified with the bass parts on hits by the Supremes, Marvin Gaye, Wilson Pickett, and others, zeroing in on the lines laid down by James Jamerson and Jerry Jemmott, among others. In rock, he found Jimi Hendrix especially inspirational, along with bassists Jack Bruce, Harvey Brooks, Jack Casady, and Noel Redding. Mark adopted bass as his second instrument when he was about 13, at about the same time he began playing trumpet professionally with jazz bands, orchestras, and R&B ensembles.

His love of scuba diving prompted him to enter the University of Miami's oceanography program, but during the summer prior to entering college he decided that music, not science, was his true calling, so he enrolled in the music program. At Miami, he met future bandmates, including Danny Gottlieb, Pat Metheny, and Clifford Carter, as well as guitarists Stan Samole and Hiram Bullock, drummer Bill Bowker, and saxophonist Mark Colby.

Until he started at the University, Mark had followed trumpeters such as Clark Terry, Miles Davis, and Clifford Brown, and listened primarily to R&B and mainstream jazz. His tastes broadened through exposure to avant-garde forms and the many styles indigenous to the Miami area, and he played in an improvisational ensemble called the South Dade, as well as in Afro-Cuban and Caribbean bands. "The nice thing about Miami," Egan observes, "is that it truly is a melting pot." As a trumpet major for the first year-and-a-half, he played in wind ensembles and jazz bands, and moonlighted on club dates around Miami Beach. He jammed on bass with friends and was asked by Mark Colby if he'd fill in on bass for a club gig. Because he knew the songs on trumpet, it was only a matter of transposing them for bass. The job became steady employment, and Mark eventually changed his major to bass.

Egan remained at Miami for six years and received a Bachelor's degree in applied music. After a year of graduate school, though, he quit to pursue a career as a performer. In 1975, Mark joined horn man Ira Sullivan's band, playing alongside guitarist Joe Diorio, whose penchant for musical exploration left a lasting impression. He also ventured into R&B and reggae groups, and did TV and studio work, as well as sessions for local records.

Mark spent the next year working with singer Phyllis Hyman in a band that included Hiram Bullock,

recorded with singer Michael Franks. Between tours with Franks in '83 and '84, Mark played for the Gil Evans Big Band. Those familiar with the Pat Metheny Group know Egan and Gottlieb from their work with the guitarist between 1977 and 1980. He's toured with singer Carly Simon, pianist Eumir Deodato, Latin percussionist Airto Moreira and singer Flora Purim, and the Pointer Sisters. Between gigs, he records for TV, radio, and commercials. Currently, he has an arsenal of unusual instruments, including a 10-string bass, a doubleneck 8-string fretted/4-string fretless, and a variety of other custom models.

Born on January 14, 1951, in Brockton, Massachusetts, Mark started on guitar at age ten, but abandoned it after only a few lessons with an uninspiring teacher. The next year, he began playing trumpet at school and

Clifford Carter, Bill Bowker, and pianist Howie Schneider. The group moved to New York and broke up shortly thereafter when Bullock left to join saxophonist David Sanborn's band. The remaining players went on the road backing the Pointer Sisters, and afterwards Mark returned to New York, where he worked with Eumir Deodato, recorded with David Sanborn on his *Promise Me The Moon* album, and began studying upright bass with jazz man Dave Holland, whom Mark credits with developing his right- and left-hand applications and his approach to improvisation.

In 1977, Pat Metheny invited Mark to play a trio gig in Niack, New York, with Danny Gottlieb. Shortly afterwards, Pat left vibraphonist Gary Burton's band and joined forces with keyboardist Lyle Mays, Gottlieb, and Egan to form the Pat Metheny Group, with whom Mark worked for three-and-a-half years. With them, he focused his attention primarily on fretless bass, and recorded *The Pat Metheny Group* and *American Garage*. The quartet toured for nearly 300 days a year and became one of the most acclaimed modern instrumental jazz bands.

Upon departing Metheny's group in 1980, Mark went on the road with singer Carly Simon. He spent the next year working with Airto Moreira and Flora Purim, as well as doing gigs with clarinetist Stan Getz, Larry Coryell, and Bill Connors. In 1983, he reunited with Danny Gottlieb to form Elements. In the following interview, he discusses his unusual custom instruments, the importance of strong musical roots, and his approach to enhancing solo bass through multiple harmonies and electronic processing.

* * * *

*D*oes working with many different kinds of musicians improve your abilities, or does it scatter your energies?*

It strengthens my individual direction. I think it's good to have a strong identity of who you are and what your playing is, so that you don't get too dispersed. Playing with a lot of great players inspired me in my own music. But I also think you have to have a strong direction from within.

Some musicians lose their individuality after spending a long time in the studio or working outside of their own field.

Well, for myself, studio work is a means for a living that allows me to have time to be creative. It's creative, but it also means that I don't have to go out on the road all the time, and I can work on my own music with Elements. That's my main focus, as far as my musical statement or expression goes, because we do whatever we want to do. And I think our two albums are probably the best representations of my playing.

Songs such as "Color Wheel" [Elements] *sound as if they're in unusual time signatures, and in some songs the harmonics take on strange sonorities.*

"Color Wheel" is basically sextuplets over a 4/4. But there's another tune on that record, "Electric Field," which was an 8-string bass with a *D* string dropped to a *C* and the *E* string raised to an *F*; the pairs of strings were then tuned in fifths. So, the harmonics are ridiculous.

How did you get into 8-string bass?

I played a Hagstrom while I was in Miami. My bass teacher, Don Coffman, had one, and I thought it was nice at the time, although it seemed like more of a specialty instrument—it didn't have that good a feel. Then, when I was in Japan with Pat Metheny, Ibanez presented me with an 8-string that felt great. It had a really good sound, and I started to fool around with that. It got me started on these exotic instruments. Now, a lot of my instruments are either made by Ibanez or Mike Pedulla, a custom bass maker from Massachusetts. I have several Pedulla basses; Mike's great, he's helped me out a lot. He built me a 10-string, which is essentially a 5-string with each one doubled, an 8-string fretless with an amazing sound, a double-neck 8-string fretted/4-string fretless, a 4-string fretless, a 4-string fretted, and a 5-string fretless. I also have Ibanez MC924 fretted and fretless basses and an Ibanez 8-string fretted, plus a Morch 5-string from Germany. Actually, I have more than that, but those are the basic ones that I play.

Does the added tension of ten strings cause tuning problems?

No. My first one had some neck trouble, but since then I've gotten a new Pedulla, and it's great; the neck stays totally straight. I like ebony boards. I like the density. It adds strength to the neck, it's more resilient, and it gives more sustain. It really makes a fretless sing, too. I basically tune the 10-string from low *E* up to *C* and in octaves. On the solo record, I get to use a lot of these instruments, and on the next Elements record it will be basses loaded [*laughs*]. Together, these instruments offer a whole spectrum of sound.

With as many outside projects as you and Danny have, how do you keep Elements going?

First of all, Danny and I are basically the band—the conceptual stuff—even though Bill and Cliff contribute their artistry. But, we're always in touch, talking about it and thinking about what we're going to do next. The concept behind Elements is to keep it as creative and uncompromising as possible. None of it was intended to be specifically commercial. It's exactly what we wanted, and I think our music has been successful in that it's been well received.

Do you use effects very much?

Yes, I have a very elaborate system. Over the last couple of years, I've really gotten into the use of effects to create ambient situations—to simulate a valley or being in a large room or hall. My approach is to enhance the sound, rather than to make it a foreign kind of sound.

So, you're trying to create an illusion of size and location?

Exactly, although sometimes I like to change the timbre, too. I also decided to get the best equipment, because I'm called to play melodies or do harmonics on certain tunes, such as with Le Bon and Rhodes. I have a Lexicon 200 Digital Reverb and two Lexicon PCM 42 digital delays with extended memory, an Ibanez Harmonics/Delay—which is great—an ADA STD-1 Stereo Tapped Delay, a T.C. Electronics Stereo Chorus/Flanger, a DeArmond volume pedal, and some Ibanez rack-mounted multi-effects units with a stereo chorus, flanger, and analog delay. For amplification, I use two Walter Wood amps—a 300-watt and a 120-watt—and two Carvin amps with two speaker cabinets containing an Electro-Voice 15″ speaker each. I also use Tiel cabinets with one 15 each; I got them in Boston at Wurlitzer. They're great. I go in quad, with my cabinets in a semi-circle around Danny. I feed the delays into the amps left-right/left-right.

Are the majority of your studio calls for fretless?

Lately, it's been about even between the two. A lot of people call me specifically to do fretless, and other calls are for generic Fender sounds. I like playing fretted bass, as well as funk and hard rock. I have a classic 1964 Fender Jazz Bass for those dates. I'm not a purist; I don't always have to play fretless. I do whatever is called for, to make it the best I can.

On some of Elements' songs, such as "Heartlake" [Forward Motion], a synthesizer plays below the bass' range. When the synth provides the low end, how does that affect your approach to the piece?

I want what the music calls for. On that song, we wanted a huge bass sound—basically an Oberheim

synthesizer sound. I intended it to free me to play a melody on top of it. As a matter of fact, that's one of the things that I love about playing with Clifford Carter; we switch functions where he'll play Minimoog bass and I'll play melody. I like that because it frees you to do other things. Also, the sound of synth bass totally fits the character of the tune, whereas if it were just electric bass, it might not be exactly the right sound. To me, it's an orchestrational thing. If I want monstrous bass, we'll use a synth, and then I'll play on top of it—or maybe I won't play at all. I don't always have to play on Elements records.

Are you interested in bass guitar-style synthesizer controllers?

I plan to get a bass synthesizer trigger as soon as one's available that lets you plug any bass into any synthesizer. At first, I thought, "Well, I'll just sound like every other synthesizer player." But if you apply your musical knowledge and taste to whatever instrument you play, whether you pick up a flute or anything else, it's still going to be you. From a compositional and orchestrational standpoint, I'm looking forward to it. I want to remain as open as I can, so that I can play as much music as possible.

You were given a lot of room to stretch out on Bill Evans' album.

Right. We were both going for conceptual records. In Elements, we don't feel like we have to play a lot of technique to get the point across, and Bill felt the same way. He just wanted to create some different waves. He didn't think he had to show off virtuosity, even though he is a virtuoso. I respect that a lot. I don't really care for records where someone's playing a lot of technique just because it's their first record.

On difficult, lengthy songs like Evans' "Living In The Crest Of A Wave" and the Metheny Group's "The Epic" [American Garage], how do you maintain your stamina and endurance?

It's like running a marathon: You can't suddenly run a 20-miler after not running for a year. You build up to it. My stamina comes from playing a lot, so by the time I actually do something, I've worked up to it.

Do you practice much?

I usually don't follow a particular routine, but I do try to play every day. When I do sit down to practice, I go through different routines. I take out some Bach violin sonatas and partitas and read through them. I don't play them at the tempo they're written at because they're written for violin at high speed. But from a harmonic point of view, it's such solid foundation harmony. Then I sometimes practice scales or improvisation, or I just turn on the metronome and work on right-hand exercises involving different combinations of strings.

The right-hand is often neglected in favor of left-hand technique.

That's right. And if you focus on your right hand, you can eliminate a lot of stumbling blocks and have much more consistency. Then, when you have a line to play, you don't fall into a trap where you have to do it a certain way. In other words, if I'm learning a melody, I play it in all different positions with the left hand, and try all sorts of left- and right-hand combinations. Sometimes I isolate the left hand and play scales on one string with it, and sometimes I just do hammer-on or trill exercises with the left hand for strength. It depends on how much time I have. If I have a block of about a week where it looks like I'm not going to be that busy, I set up a daily routine. It really takes repetition and discipline to get ahead, practice-wise. And I've gone through a lot of that—especially when I was in Miami and early on in New York, when I was practicing fanatically, six hours a day. It's a constant thing; it's going to be like that for life, and you just have to get used to that fact if you want to take it as far as you can.

Where do you derive your inspiration for Elements?

A lot of it comes from Kauai, Hawaii. Danny and I have friends there, and we've spent a lot of time out there playing duo; the whole band was there about a year ago. It's a real magical place for us. A friend has a house in a valley, and I borrowed a bunch of amps, set up a power generator—there's no electricity otherwise—and we played all night. It was definitely one of the highest musical experiences of our lives.

Do you feel that the places where people play have an effect on their approach?

I think it's an individual thing; everyone is affected by their environment. If you are in a positive one, or where there are progressive people around, it's going to enhance whatever you do, whether it's in the stock market, music, or whatever. And I think if you're in paradise—which Hawaii is—you can't help but be inspired, unless you have some serious problems. It's important to always be in the most positive environment possible. Positive to some people can be hanging out at a pizza parlor, and that's fine for them. It's all a matter of what your inner feelings say to you.

What made you want to record a solo album?

I had been playing a lot of solo with all my new effects that I had acquired, and I felt the need to crys-

talize that point in time. We recorded it in November '84. It's all original tunes with a lot of the Elements influence in it. Three of the pieces are entirely solo bass with a lot of overdubs. The whole thing was orchestrated on manuscript paper the way you would orchestrate a big band. I played all the parts, and I got a chance to really use my instruments—a full spectrum from the 8-string to the 4-string to the 5-string fretless. It was amazingly challenging because it was basically me alone. I had to come up with a lot of the input myself, although [producer] Steve Miller was a tremendous help for guidance.

How did the airy sound of "Valley Hymn" come about?

That was actually inspired while I was playing in the valley in Hawaii. I had the amplifiers all around me in a semi-circle, and I was playing the doubleneck; at one point, the wind was actually playing the strings while I fingered the chords. That whole piece was recorded without overdubs. I used about eight different banks of stereo delays in the studio. The first set of PCM-42s were set to about 500 milliseconds and 1,000, then 1,500 and 2,000, so everything just kept regenerating. In the end, I had the Lexicon 224 Digital Reverb set to give a lot of reverb.

How did you approach the Le Bon and Rhodes sessions?

Mostly like a rock and roll situation, but after we did a few takes, Nick Rhodes said, "Listen you guys, stretch out. We want you to be experimental." I thought that was fantastic; it sort of set the pace for the whole project. It was a real challenge, and the only guideline that I had was a chord sheet. Nothing else was written, actually.

Had you ever desired to play on a hit record?

I've been on some *great* records with Pat Metheny and Elements, and artistically I couldn't ask for anything more. But I also wanted to be on something that was played a lot all over the world, that reached a lot of people. I think this new record with Simon and Nick may be even bigger than Duran Duran because it will reach a more adult-oriented audience. There's also talk of a possible promotional tour—maybe even promotional videos that I might be involved in.

That would be a whole new realm.

Definitely. A lot of doors are opening up for me now. I feel fortunate to have these opportunities, and I feel like a lot of the hard work has paid off—and there's a lot of hard work ahead. I always want to keep that attitude because I want to keep growing. One of my big inspirations is John McLaughlin, who's an all-time constant musician. He's just someone I really admire. Also, Jascha Heifetz, the violinist, is one of my idols. I've got some movies that he made, I read his biographies, and I've got about everything he's ever recorded. I think when you surround yourself with music by masters, surround yourself with a real high level of whatever it is your pursuing, it can only lift you up and bring you closer to it.

If I can offer anything to players, it's to surround yourself with the best possible artists who are doing the type of music you want to play. It only makes sense. And also, just give some thought to a general education in music. I can't exaggerate the importance of having strong roots and having a firm background and knowledge of the music you're trying to learn. You've got to have a strong foundation. Young players must see that it's important to study the masters and really check out what's happening. I think it's good in the beginning to emulate other players. Look at someone like Eric Clapton or Hendrix or Miles or [saxophonists] John Coltrane or Charlie Parker, who all spent a lot of time listening to their favorite players of whatever style—they could probably sing and play every note of it at one time. You have to latch onto something at some point. You can't just start in the closet. At the same time, you want your own style, and you don't want to get hung up sounding like someone else. Remember, copying someone else is a stepping stone. I feel strongly about this. I'm still trying to get the roots together. If you want to become the best, you've got to be around the best.

I understand you come from a strong multi-directional background.

Fortunately, I was part of the baby boom generation, and I grew up listening to the Beatles, Hendrix, Miles, and avant-garde music. All those influences come out. I don't feel like I'm a jazz player or a rock player. It's funny that after recording with Simon Le Bon and Nick Rhodes, *Rolling Stone* identified me as a jazz bassist. Am I a jazz bassist? To people who just play rock and don't improvise at all, I guess I'm a jazz player, relatively speaking. But I would rather be thought of as a multi-directional player. I hate terms; I hate to be classified. I'm definitely into improvisational music. I've worked hard at developing that craft, and to me it's really important to be able to express myself on the instrument. And through improvisation, I have avenues to express myself. □

A Selected Mark Egan Discography
Solo album: *Mosaic*, Hip Pocket (dist. by Windham Hill), HP 104. **With Elements:** *Elements*, Antilles (dist. by Island), AN 1017; *Forward Motion*, Antilles, AN 1021. **With Michael Franks:** *Objects Of Desire*, Warner Bros., BSK 3648; *Skindive*, Warner Bros., 1-25275. **With the Pat Metheny Group:** *Pat Metheny Group*, ECM, ECM-1-1114; *American Garage*, ECM, ECM-1-1155. **With others:** David Sanborn, *Promise Me The Moon*, B-3051; Bill Evans, *Living In The Crest Of A Wave*, Elektra/Musician, 9 60349-1-E.

Bass Solo From "Baby Bossa'

By Mark Egan

The intention behind "Baby Bossa" [from Elements' *Forward Motion*] was to create a simple, melodic, Brazilian-influenced composition. It was inspired by my niece and written on the bass. When Danny Gottlieb and I were preparing for the *Forward Motion* album, the tune was chosen as a feature for the fretless bass, as well as a vehicle for Clifford Carter's keyboard improvisations. The chord changes are included, in case you want to play this with a guitarist or keyboardist. Compound chord symbols with a slash separating two parts (for example, *B7/A*) indicate the chord to be played followed by the lowest note.

MICHAEL HEDGES

By Mark Hanson and Phil Hood

Frets, November 1986

Impossible! I can't believe that's only one guitar!'' Such exclamations are common among people hearing Michael Hedges' guitar playing, for the first time. Not since Leo Kottke's debut album (*6- and 12-String Guitar,* [Takoma, out of print]) have so many acoustic guitar aficionados reacted as strongly to a new artist. Michael Hedges gets people's attention.

A powerful rhythmic player, with the touch and sensitivity of a trained classical guitarist, Hedges is causing a major rethinking of the solo steel-string guitar's capabilities. With his unique chordal style, Hedges' playing does indeed at times sound like two—or even three—guitars. The fact that his first three albums were basically recorded "live" is a testament to his considerable talents as a composer and an innovator in guitar technique.

The foundation of Hedges' guitar work is his unwavering sense of rhythm. From the percussive rock beat of ''Hot Type'' to the reflective lyricism of ''Lenono,'' Hedges plays with a masterful command of tempo and phrasing. His harmonic inventiveness is just as masterful, going one step beyond most of today's open-tuning fingerstylists. He seldom plays in the more common open tunings, preferring to alter them, or to invent new ones compatible with his latest harmonic concepts.

Though his technique is formidable, Hedges himself downplays its importance in his music. He favors unusual open tunings not only to create new voicings, he says, but also to make his tunes easier to play. To coax as much sound as possible out of his guitar, he uses two-hand tapping, harmonics, and simultaneous but totally independent left- and right-hand techniques.

Except for a three-second splice of acoustic guitar at the beginning of ''Silent Anticipations,'' everything on his first all-instrumental guitar album, *Breakfast In The Field,* was recorded with no overdubbing. The record put the world of acoustic guitar on notice that a new major talent was on the scene.

His second instrumental release, *Aerial Boundaries,* established Hedges as one of today's most inventive acoustic guitarists. Hedges augmented his guitar compositions with flute, and a variety of tape techniques. The third and most recent Hedges album, *Watching My Life Go By,* showcases Hedges as a songwriter and a singer as well as a guitarist.

Musically educated at Peabody Institute in Baltimore, Maryland, Hedges is proficient on flute, piano, and bass, in addition to guitar. With several directions open to him for his next recording projects, Hedges talked with *Frets* at his studio in Palo Alto, California, about his music, and his hopes for its development in the future.

* * * *

When did you really start to develop your style?

There wasn't really a starting point; I feel like it will never really begin or end, I hope. I don't want to be limited by what people call a *style.* I want to write music as I feel it, not what people expect of me because of what I've done in the past. I'd like to make a record of chamber music where I don't even play guitar; and I'd like to make a full-fledged rock album. I just want to be a musician. Guitar doesn't really matter that much, except that it is a lot of fun to play. But I have a great time doing other things, too, as long as it's music. I just don't want to be pigeonholed.

How did your use of alternate guitar tunings evolve?

I think I started playing around with tunings when ''Suite: Judy Blue Eyes'' came out [*Crosby, Stills and Nash,* Atlantic, 19117]. It's a great tuning, *D A D D A D,* I think. [*Ed. Note: The actual tuning for ''Suite: Judy Blue Eyes'' on the first C, S & N album was* E B E E B E.] I played a lot of Neil Young songs in bars over the years, using his tunings. Double-*D*-down [*D A D G B D, lowest pitch to highest*] for instance [*plays Young's ''When You Dance I Can Really Love,'' from* After the Gold Rush *(Reprise, K-2283)*]. That kind of thing really

got me into the heavy-strum, Neil Young type of rhythmic style in my playing.

Do you use special string gauges to accommodate your tunings?

I use .013, .017, .026, .034, .046, and .056. Those are the gauges where my tunings work.

Your music is very chordal. Do your tunings evolve out of a set of chord changes that you want to work from, or a melody that you hear?

Most of the time it's a chord that I really like the voicing of, and that I can't get in any other configuration. And I like stuff that is easy to play, because then I can just forget about the technique. That's one reason that I use alternate tunings—just to make stuff easier to play. And I love the sound of open strings, which explains why I have really gotten into harp guitar recently. It has the longest string length available for the pitches. I like the sound of the long strings.

How do you decide what pitches you will use for the bass strings of the harp guitar?

I have this tune I play on my Dyer guitar with *G Bb*

C A D as the bass line. I tuned them in this order because that way I could mute them with my right hand, using rest strokes. Once I got familiar with that tuning, I started writing another tune, and for that one I changed maybe one string.

Do you ever use standard tuning?

No, I don't. I improvise in standard tuning on an electric when I do fills and stuff, but I don't really want to do that. I think that I am headed for being able to improvise in my own tunings—kind of like Pierre Bensusan does in "Dadgad" tuning [*D A D G A D*, lowest pitch to highest]. I still know the fretboard better in standard tuning than in my own tunings for improvising single lines. I think Pierre's brain is just wired differently.

You have a broad musical education. How has that helped you?

I went to Peabody Institute in Baltimore and tried to get through the standard repertoire of classical guitar, which I could never play as well as [classical virtuoso] Angel Romero. Could you? If you were into

other things as much as classical guitar, would you spend as much as six hours a day on classical guitar? [*Laughs.*] I was really into steel-string too. I was playing in a blues band two nights a week, and on weekends I was playing a solo vocal gig with steel-string. I had a French class every morning at eight after I had been playing until three, so I couldn't spend six hours a day on classical guitar. What I *could* do was spend four hours a day composing, so I switched majors. I was trying to do a double major—composition and guitar—but after two years I switched to just composition and gave a senior recital, all of which was freely atonal stuff for ensemble. Only one piece was for guitar. The recital was chamber music, all written out. I wrote all of it on the piano, then orchestrated it. I learned all of that getting my degree.

Do you notate your own pieces?

No, the guitar pieces are easy enough to remember. I'll make tapes so I don't forget ideas. Right before I recorded *Aerial Boundaries* I wrote everything out note-for-note so I could look at it while I rehearsed. That really helped my phrasing.

Did you change anything in the process of writing out the music?

No. Things just became clearer in my mind when I was playing them. I compose completely by ear and sound. I don't make too much stuff up in my head. I usually have to experiment and hear things. That's why

I call my publishing company Naked Ear. It's not really supposed to be too stylistic—it's supposed to be open to almost any persuasion. I don't mean to say that my music is fusion, a little of this and a little of that. I just want it to be very organic, unified.

How do you compose?

It happens different ways. I have the training of a classical composer, and I enjoy working on new ideas, experimenting with them, organizing, making all the decisions that composers make. You develop your harmonic sense, and then figure out ways to develop a theme or an idea with that. For example, I could have an idea that is non-guitar based—maybe there's a chordal progression that I come up with on the piano. To put it on the guitar I may have to simplify it or re-voice it a bit. I work a lot on the piano. The piano has a freer type of layout; guitar is more restricted in chord voicing because you only have six strings. So I'm used to working with inspirations other than guitar.

What instruments besides piano provide those inspirations?

I really like mountain dulcimer, the way they tune a lot of the strings to unison pitches. I've been doing a lot of that lately. My latest guitar thing, which we'll make into a single for the next record, has this tuning: C G D G G G, lowest pitch to highest [*plays part of a very percussive instrumental*]. You have to tune the open strings a little strangely to compensate for the different gauges. One stretches a little more than another when you fret them up the neck; so in order to get them in tune up the neck, you have to have them a little *out* of tune when they are open. Hearing all the unisons in Irish music has been influential in my composing. They tune their guitars in "Dadgad" a lot. But I try to add one note that is a little more colorful. That's kind of like my crusade, I guess. I just want to hear new voicings. And I don't mind retuning my guitar [during performance] to get a new voicing. When I'm onstage I'll use the applause to cover me while I'm going to the new intervals. And then I use some kind of story or chatter while I get the fine tuning.

Do you try to convey the sense of the lyrics in the music of the songs that you write?

My music is not always text painting. Lots of time it's more like, 'Here, I've got this music; now let's put some words to it,' and I'll try to make it fit. It doesn't always have to go together exactly. If you are singing about sweet birds and flowers, it doesn't have to be sweet music.

What do you tell people on the road when they ask

you what you call your music?

I'm really a folkie, but I hate to say "folk music," because folk music is sort of dead in the record stores. It's not good for business. So I'll just say that I play original guitar solos, and I like rock a lot. And then my albums make the *Billboard* jazz charts!

Your material sounds as though Joni Mitchell has had a big influence on you.

She's my favorite singer-songwriter. Part of it is that I'm singing over these open-tuning guitar chords. That's why Elliot Mazer, the producer of my vocal album, wouldn't let me use the fretless bass on the record. He was afraid that people would peg me for Joni, with that Jaco Pastorius fretless bass sound. I really wanted to have Mike Manring play on the album, so he played fretted bass instead. Joni and David Crosby really got me into tunings. Did you ever hear Crosby's solo album, *If Only I Could Remember My Name* [Atlantic, 7203]? It was wonderful, and he was the one who taught Joni how to play with open tunings on the guitar.

Did you listen to strictly instrumental guitarists as well as singer/songwriters back then?

Oh. Yeah. Martin Carthy, Leo Kottke, Willis Ramsey, some John Renbourn. Lately I've been listening to a lot of Celtic music. Pierre Bensusan. Early Bruce Cockburn. About four albums ago I was really into Bruce. His current stuff is too political for me, but I still love him. I listen to John Martyn a lot. He really got me into slapping. Then there's Willis Ramsey, who wrote "Muskrat Love." I play every song that Willis ever wrote. He's one of my favorite people, but he's the most reclusive guy I have ever met. I chased him down in Texas, and had him teach his songs to me. I had a neighbor who played his records all the time, back in Arizona about '72. Willis' album came out in '70 or '71. He hasn't made one since. He's still living off the royalties of "Muskrat Love." America recorded it and made him some money. Then the Captain and Tennille recorded it and made him rich—because he owns his own publishing; all of it.

How did you begin working out your string-tapping technique?

My initial aim with the tapping technique was the *sound*. I wanted that really percussive sound. But my tapping was dictated by technique, too. If my left hand couldn't reach a note that I wanted, I would tap with my right hand to get it. Later on it changed to where tapping was dictated by the music instead. It was a texture that my imagination wanted at certain points in the music. More recently, I've often wanted more counterpoint than I can get with the standard technique of one hand fretting and one hand picking, and the only way to get it is by fretting separate notes with each hand.

When did you really start using left-hand percussive techniques?

It happened when I wrote "Silent Anticipations."

Do you ever hit the guitar with your wedding ring?

No. The ring is too much. The reason you hear so much percussion is because of the Frap pickup that I use inside the guitar.

What do you do when you break a fingernail?

Use artificial nails; or get a thick ping-pong ball, and cut pieces out of it. That works. I was on my way to a concert in L.A. and was scared I was going to lose a nail, because one had a nick in it. So we stopped and got a ping-pong ball. I felt better all night. Get a good quality one; they are hard to find after business hours!

What harp guitars are you currently playing?

I have two Dyers, and I just got this Gibson with 11 harp strings. Neil Penner in Enid, Oklahoma, found it for me.

Do you try to avoid the sympathetic vibrations from the bass strings of the harp guitar?

I have to really watch it. But the sympathetic ones I don't mind. Even with a regular 6-string you have one or two strings vibrating sympathetically anyway. With a harp guitar there are just more of them. With certain kinds of bass lines, sometimes I have to mute a bass string when I pluck an adjacent one, so the two low frequencies don't conflict. There is more of a muting problem than a sympathetic vibration problem. I like the sympathetic vibrations.

Are you using the harp guitar bass strings in the same way you previously were using the low strings on the standard guitar?

Not really, because I do like to do bass runs on them. And I couldn't really do bass runs on the 6-string, in the style I was playing, and have it sound good to me. I didn't want it to sound like a scale being played on the guitar. I wanted it to sound a little bit more legato. I know what it is—it's because the harp guitar's strings are all the same string length; and they are all open. That's the sound I was looking for, but I have to really mute them. It gets muddy if one note sustains into the next.

You produced yourself on your first two albums. Whose decision was it to bring in Elliot Mazer for Watching My Life Go By*?*

Elliot called me and said that he wanted to produce it. I thought it was great. He did Neil Young's *Harvest* album [Reprise, MKS-2277], and he knows how to get that real acoustic sound; and I think he succeeded. It's not a pop record. It's a very eclectic record with strange-tuned folk songs. And some of them aren't really *pleasing* in the folk style. The folk ones are in a new kind of style. I'm pretty happy with the record, although some people don't think it was produced right. I think it was produced just fine: It was exactly what I wanted to do. It just didn't sell a whole lot of copies, that's all. It's only sold about 45,000, compared to 115,000 for *Aerial Boundaries*, and about 100,000 for *Breakfast in the Field*. But it paid for itself. It's keeping me on the road. All of those songs were several years old, except for "Face Yourself" and the new arrangement of "All Along the Watchtower." I was really happy to get that stuff out of the way. As a songwriter with too many old songs around, it's very hard on your self-image. Especially when you're a guitar player, and people are waiting for you to make a fool out of yourself by singing. It's a very psychological kind of thing when you go out to make a vocal album after two strong instrumental albums. I was very scared, and that's where Elliot really helped out. He's used to working with artists. He knows they are kind of psycho.

As a fingerstylist, do you have to adapt your solo style when you play with a band?

No. I get bands together mostly to augment my material. I'm arranging a new tune for a band. The bass player is playing my bass line exactly. It's just doubled. It adds that depth. He's doing a lot of slap, funky kind of stuff. The drummer is doing a real simple bass drum and backbeat. Those are my criteria for a band. They have to flow out of what I am doing. And that way it will be my arrangement. In a way, they become extensions of my guitar. That's the way I want to approach it. That way I can get a pretty original type of arrangement.

Do you have any advice for beginning guitarists?

I think guitarists in general should play with other musicians, for their rhythmic stability. I love playing rhythm guitar. It's one of the harder things to do. A lot of the people that I've taught need to be in some kind of ensemble. If you are used to playing solo guitar, it's great to play with a band, even if you aspire to playing strictly solo, later. I play drums now to help my guitar playing, simply because I want to hone-in on tempos—subtle tempo changes between sections. I'm talking about tempo changes, and how they can be used effectively. Leo Kottke does that really well.

What is the secret of doing that well?

I talked with him about it, and he said that he listened to harpsichord players, who *have* to use tempo changes to affect the music because they don't have any dynamics to play with in the instrument. [*Ed. Note: The harpsichord mechanism, unlike that of a piano or clavichord, does not allow a player to express dynamics. No matter how hard a key is struck, the action plucks the related string with a constant force.*] Get your rhythm together and you can play the easiest stuff in the world and it will sound great. It's also a lot easier to practice. You just *sound* better. Tone is important, too. Not enough people pay attention to it.

How does a player go about getting better tone?

I think everybody ought to study classical guitar, if they want to be a guitar player. Getting a good tone on a classical guitar is something to be learned. If you eventually want to play steel-string or anything, practice your single strings. Learn what a good tone sounds like. Find out what you are capable of doing; and then if you can make *every* note that you play sound as good as that, you'll really have it. I spent a good five years studying classical guitar—two summers and three full years I studied at Peabody. I was taking a lesson each week and was expected to practice several hours a day. I didn't practice that much, mostly because I had to go backward and practice just one string. I was aching to play music, but I couldn't at first because my tone wasn't up to their standards. But it was good to learn all the classical techniques—rest stroke and free stroke—stuff that I still use a lot. People think that my music is mostly special effects, but I am a real believer in learning the classical way of doing things. Then you can forget it if you want; but you can always come back to it if you need it. You at least have some sort of foundation that is pretty well developed.

Is that something that you can study on your own? Are there any particularly good methods to follow?

A Selected Michael Hedges Discography
Solo albums: *Watching My Life Go By*, Open Air, (dist. by RCA), OA-0303; (on Windham Hill): *Breakfast In The Field*, 1017; *Aerial Boundaries*, 1032; *Live On The Double Planet*, 1066. **With others** (on Windham Hill): *Sampler '82*, WH-1024; *Windham Hill Records Sampler '84*, WH6-1035.

The guitar doesn't have nearly as codified a system of playing as does the piano or other string instruments, like violin. There are so many different ways that people teach guitar. But I think some type of classical training is really going to help out, even if you don't wind up playing in that style. It's a method of getting yourself disciplined. Or even if you study yoga or something, it's still a method of getting the concentration that is necessary to play music. Explore your sense of rhythm. Learn what a good tone is. If you can just play in a groove, you still can have a good time, even if the music is simple. □

"Layover"

By Michael Hedges

by Mark Hanson

"Layover' is about the closest I get to playing a regular alternating bass style," says Michael Hedges. That makes "Layover" one of the more readily accessible 6-string guitar pieces in Hedges repertoire, and it's transcribed here as a sampler of some of his distinctive techniques. Measures 5 through 24 use a nearly constant alternating-bass pattern. In measures 25-38, the alternating bass disappears, and continual one-, two-, and three-string hammer-ons ("tapping") are introduced.

To ensure bright harmonics in measures 12-14, finger the 7th fret of the third string with the *index* finger; and the fourth-string harmonic with the *middle* finger. In measures 29 and 30, Hedges emphasizes the *lower-pitched* of the two simultaneously-plucked notes in the top voice—a difficult technique, but a necessary one to bring out the melody. The guitar tuning is *D A C G C E*, lowest pitch to highest.

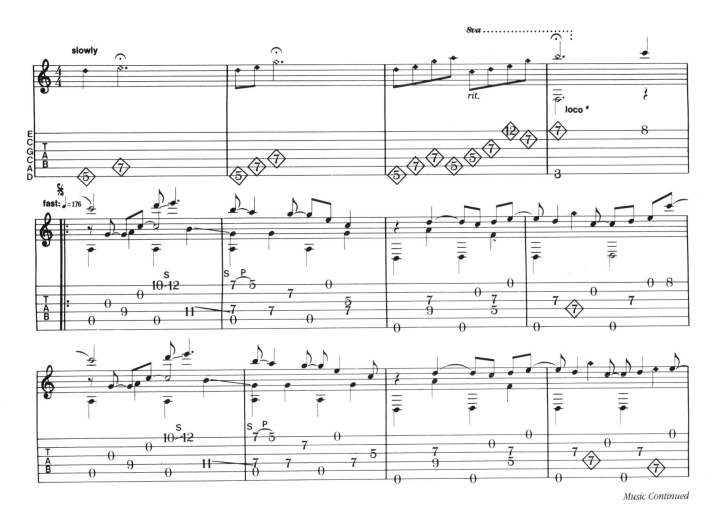

Music Continued

Continued From Previous Page

MICHAEL HOENIG

By Ted Greeenwald

Keyboard, March 1988

Nearly a decade after giving up the idea of being a recording artist, electronic pioneer Michael Hoenig found himself with a compelling reason to make a record: Out of the blue, a record company actually asked him for an album. No demo tapes, no pounding the pavement, no sacrifice of artistic vision; Cinema Records, a new label dedicated to probing the stylistic intersections between new age and progressive rock, called *him.*

"They convinced me that they loved my music," the affable German synthesist, a former member of Tangerine Dream who released a solo album in 1978 and was featured in *Keyboard*'s January 1979 issue, explains. "When they told me about the concept of the label, I was very frank in saying, 'Well, I'm really trying to achieve something in other areas now.' But they seemed so convinced that I said, 'Hey, if someone feels that good about it, maybe I should try it again.' And that's how it really happened."

Cinema's faith in Hoenig bore fruit with *Xcept One* [CLT-46919], an involving collection in which the mechanistic pulses of modern sequencing hurtle headlong into the glistening, reflective pools of the new age. The composer's longtime fascination with Steve Reich-style compositional processes, hocket patterns, and metrical ambiguities is given a turbo-charged shot of electronic percussion in "Scatter Part I," "Scatter Part II," and "Bones On The Beach," while quiet soundscapes such as "Forgotten Thoughts" and "Spectral Gong," both collaborations with Harold Budd, explore more somber moods.

The call to create *Xcept One* interrupted Hoenig in the midst of what had become a protracted exploration of the music-industry niches most commonly occupied by talented professionals hoping to escape the vagaries of the record business. "In 1979, when I got the axe from Warner Bros., I was rather frustrated with the record industry," he recalls. "There didn't seem to be room for what I was doing, other than on small, independent labels that I didn't want to get involved with

because I just didn't want to find my music only in bookstores and health food stores. So I began to explore other fields of music."

Hoenig's explorations soon settled into an oscillation between the avant-garde and the industrial that continues to this day. In 1980, he landed a job with experimental film director Godfrey Reggio organizing and supplementing Philip Glass' monumental score for *Koyaanisqatsi.* "It was a collaborative effort, and I was involved in every step, from the dramatic conception to the editing to the music. It was really wonderful, not only as a cinematic experience, but as a way to learn more about how much music can do to images, and vice-versa."

Hoenig put the experience to use over the next two years, scoring made-for-TV movies in the U.S. before returning to Germany for a year. In 1983, he left Europe and established a permanent studio in Los Angeles. There, he became involved with film composer Jack Nietsche, producing Nietsche's scores for *9½ Weeks* and *Jewel Of The Nile.* He also scored the ill-fated *Max Headroom* TV series.

"Working in the movie industry is a little bit like working for the Post Office," Hoenig jokes. "You have to work your way up. You do some really crummy work, and then sometimes some good stuff sprinkles in. Then some real good stuff comes along, and then for a long time nothing happens. But if you're persistent, it grows."

The fringes of the record industry also began to beckon: Hoenig's production credits expanded to include works by such visionaries as Morton Subotnick and Harold Budd. Hoenig is hesitant to define his role as producer for such artists. "It's hard for me to talk about my contribution," he states. "I can deliver on the final recording, I hope, what their ideas are all about. You know, there are producers who understand an awful lot about pop music, and how to make relatively mediocre songs appear sensational. Obviously, they have some tricks, or something that you could call craft, that composers and recording engineers don't necessarily have. My role is really a bridge between those two things [composition and engineering]."

Still, working with so-called serious composers requires a different set of priorities than producing a pop song. "It entirely depends on the talent of the composer on which level the producer should get involved," he observes. "You don't have to tell Morton Subotnick what note is wrong."

Ironically, it was Hoenig's work as a film composer, rather than as a record producer, that attracted Cinema's attention and determined the flavor of much of *Xcept One*. A demo created for the film *Quicksilver* (scored, in the end, by Tony Banks of Genesis) caught the ears of Cinema executives, so Hoenig went to work developing it into a finished piece. While previously he had found the record industry stifling, the challenge of transforming music created to accompany a visual image into a piece that could stand on its own struck his fancy. "It's so different," he muses, "doing music that serves the purposes of the movie, and then doing a record again, which has to hold up entirely on its own. It was hard and very painstaking, but it was a lovely thing to do."

Among the more obviously painstaking pieces on the record are "Scatter Part I" and "Scatter Part III," a pair of hard-driving ruminations on the interrelations among musical patterns. Both compositions bear a distinct rock flavor, although the drums that propel the two pieces were something of an afterthought. "You know, I'm not Mr. Beat," Hoenig admits. "The material was conceived without that element. Ralph Humphrey, who played the electronic percussion, allowed the material to appear in a different light. I didn't even know in the beginning if I would use it, but I liked a lot of what came out of it."

Drumming aside, the underlying musical materials of the two "Scatters" owe more to academic compositional techniques than to the rock tradition. Their structures arise from an almost mathematical process of combining intervals to produce melodic and metrical variations. "The music is conceived as several loops of intervals that modulate each other to create new loops of different lengths in shifting patterns," Hoenig states. "There's a loop of five [beats], of ten, of seven, and those loops intermodulate each other. Every loop shifts [the intervals of] the others at a different point in time, and then the intervals add up to different notes. It's a rather complicated process. It's almost an objective way of composing, because of the strict rules for determining the pitches."

On the other hand, the placid "Forgotten Thoughts" grew out of a more intuitive methodology. "That piece came together, really, in finding a sound, then finding one part on the left hand and then another on the right, and then laying some things over them. While it was evolving, an overall form took shape, which again was changed because it didn't work

immediately. It became an evolving process around certain sounds. I have only rare occasions in movies," he adds, "to play something that is slow and quiet and pretty."

While *Xcept One*'s jacket lists the Yamaha DX7-IIFD, Sequential Prophet-VS, Oberheim Matrix-12 and Four-Voice, Minimoog, and ARP Pro Solosit, Hoenig's primary instrument is his Synclavier. "I got the Synclavier in 1984, when it was really not at all what it is today," he reports. "But I saw possibilities in it, and I stuck with it. Now it's my main tool. At this moment in time, I think that it's the most powerful music tool that you can buy off the shelf."

Unlike most composers working with electronics, Hoenig scores every note before the production process takes place. And—surprisingly, for someone who owns a Synclavier—he scores his music by hand, complete with orchestrations. "The orchestration is always in my head," he insists. "If I hear one pattern, I hear a complete grid of things. Finding the layers that form the complete grid becomes the painstaking process, but an orchestration is an integral part of conceiving it."

Familiar orchestral timbres mingle with more imaginative sounds on *Xcept One*, but rarely do they retain their idiomatic musical functions. For instance, sampled saxophones and dark brass chords can be detected in the dramatic "Bones On The Beach," but they're mere strands in a web of hard-hitting synthesized chords, piercing upper partials, and atmospheric effects. "The usual instruments give you certain colors that make the music accessible," Hoenig observes. "Then you can introduce other things that draw people in. Then they may become more open to listen to others. I mean, I really like to work with very obscure sounds, but a record that is released on a label like Capitol [Cinema's parent company] might not be the most appropriate medium for getting really obscure things distributed to the public.

"The record had to be somewhat accessible and easy to listen to," Hoenig concludes, "but at the same time it had to leave the opportunity to add some other elements. That doesn't mean I tried to be commercial, but the elements on the record had to be sellable. I didn't try to achieve anything other than to create something that sounded fresh to my own ears," he states with an air of modest satisfaction. "What I thought was, if it's interesting for me, then it should be terrific for other people." □

MARK ISHAM

By Dominic Milano, Greg Armbruster, and
Bob Doerschuk

Introspective imagery identifies the musical textures of Mark Isham's first solo album, *Vapor
Drawings*, on the Windham Hill label. Using
synthesizers, piano, trumpet, flugelhorn, and
soprano sax, Isham weaves thought-provoking melodic
lines into a tapestry of soft contours and blending colors,
casting a subtle spell of musical mystery. His sound is not
easily pigeonholed, but his music is undeniably pleasing.

Some artists bristle when shoved into the new age
category. Mark Isham merely shrugs. "I don't mind being
called new age," he insists. "A label is a label. If people talk
about you that way, that's just fine. At least you know
that they are talking about you."

Of course, it might be just as easy to label Isham as a
jazz player, thanks to his work with pianist Art Lande. Or as

a soundtrack composer; his most recent scores, for *The
Moderns* and *The Beast Of War*, reflect the same knack for
textural and evocative writing displayed on his albums. Or
even as a rock/pop hired gun, as a result of his recent gig
on the road with David Sylvian. But there's no denying that
his latest solo LP, *Castalia*, has gotten a lot of new age
airplay. And its gauzy synthesized timbres, jazzy
touches, and gently insistent rhythms offer a textbook
example of adult contemporary music.

To some extent, Isham's lifelong interest in textures
made contact with the new age aesthetic inevitable. "The
inclination has always been there," the switch-hitting
trumpeter/synthesist admits. "As a trumpet player, I was
fairly traditional. I haven't used it to push out into new
territory, like Jon Hassel has. But as a kid sitting at the

Keyboard, December 1984 and
October 1988

piano and exploring the different moods you could create by playing chords softly, or banging the keys, or even getting inside the instrument, I was interested in how you got sounds."

Born in New York City in 1951, Isham (pronounced eye-sham) grew up in a musical household. With mother a concert violinist and father a professor of art and music, it's no wonder that Mark began violin and piano lessons at an early age. But by the time he was 13, he decided to find his own musical direction and selected the trumpet as his guide. Progressing quickly, Mark performed in junior high school stage bands and began experimenting with a broad range of trumpet styles. He explains, "My two main influences as a trumpet player were classical trumpet, the way Bach and Mahler wrote for the instrument, and jazz trumpet in the style of Miles Davis. I also liked the way [saxophonist] Wayne Shorter took a lot of those same ideas and experimented with them. None of my stylistic influences relied on flashiness or pyrotechnics. I was more interested in the quality of the sound."

When Mark's family moved to California in 1966, he tried attending the University of California at Santa Barbara but became impatient with the methodical pace of the music program and dropped out after his first year. Returning to the Bay Area, Mark did freelance work with the San Francisco and Oakland Symphonies and the San Francisco Opera. Before long, he was also gigging locally with a variety of acts, including the Sons of Champlin, the Beach Boys, Esther Phillips, Charles Lloyd, Horace Silver, Pharoah Sanders, and Dave Liebman. These jobs gave Mark considerable experience but didn't offer him the chance to explore his own musical directions. That opportunity came when he met jazz pianist Art Lande in the late 1970s.

Isham met Lande through guitarist Peter Maunu and keyboardist Mike Nock. Originally, Art, Peter, and Mark started playing free-form jazz improvisations, but they split up when Lande decided to pursue a more structured format. That didn't work out either, and when Mark and drummer Terry Bozzio approached Lande about a new band, they formed Rubisa Patrol. Bill Douglass played bass and Glenn Cronkhite added percussion and the band began to gather steam. Then Bozzio left to play with Frank Zappa, and Cronkhite shifted over to the drums. With that lineup, they recorded two albums on ECM, *Rubisa Patrol* and *Desert Ma-rauders.*

Soon after *Desert Marauders* was released, Isham left Lande and began concentrating on session work, where he met vocalist Van Morrison. Originally hired to play on one song, Mark was retained for the entire *In The Music*

album when Van Morrison discovered that Mark played more brass instruments than just piccolo trumpet. Four other albums and several tours followed as Mark's brass and synthesizer styles began to influence Morrison's sound. By the time *Inarticulate Speech Of The Heart* was released in 1983, Isham's somber synthesizer playing had become a major orchestral factor in Van Morrison's band.

During his Van Morrison association, Isham got back together with Bozzio and Maunu, and with the collaboration of bassist Patrick O'Hearn they formed Group 87. They released an album by the same name in 1981 for Columbia Records, but the band was soon dropped by the label. "We were never a live performing band," he admits. "And I think we were a little disappointed with ourselves on that first album. It felt a bit limited. After the album we put a live band together and we had a great deal of improvisation in the show." However, O'Hearn and Bozzio soon left to form the group Missing Persons, and Isham got involved with Carroll Ballard's film *Never Cry Wolf* as well as his own solo album for Windham Hill. "It's been two years since that original band fell apart," he continues, "and Peter [Maunu] and I hadn't played together for over a year until the day we started to record the new Group 87 album." Along with percussionist Peter Van Hooke, Mark and Maunu finally finished *A Career In Dada Processing* in January of 1984.

Now that Isham records for Virgin, a label whose image isn't as restrictive as Windham Hill's, he feels that he has wider stylistic options. Still, recognizing that commercial realities exist, he followed the same trail on *Castalia* that he blazed on *Vapor Drawings*, emphasizing complex electronic timbres, consonant melodies, and restraint in preference to technical fireworks. And though he acknowledges the new age inclination on both albums, Isham adds that there are differences between his philosophical approach and that of the new age purists.

To illustrate, he points to one of the softer, more filmy pieces on *Castalia.* "'In The Warmth Of Your Night' is basically a very pretty jazz ballad. There's actually a great deal of sophisticated harmony in the first part. It's rather like what Weather Report did on 'Five Short Pieces' [from *Tale Spinnin'*, Columbia, PC-33417], which were rubato pieces using the harmonic vocabularies of jazz and late Romantic or Impressionistic classical music. Nobody would think of calling them new age, because no one in Weather Report came from anything defined as a new age background."

The artist's background and musical intentions, in Isham's view, are important in assessing whether his or her work can be classified as new age. "These days there is a middle-of-the-road new age philosophy, which is that it's background music, something you can play over coffee without blowing your guests' minds. But I think that some of the most interesting and provocative ideas behind new age address the question of whether music can have an objective effect upon a person's spiritual being. All the hoopla about new age ignores the interesting question of what role music can play in real spiritual enlightenment."

Isham believes that this concern transcends simpler definitions of new age music, which tend to focus on superficial aspects of style. "I'm not a well-educated ethnomusicologist," he cautions, "but I understand that there is a lot of objective purpose in the structure of Indian music. There's the morning raga, the afternoon raga, and the evening raga, each with specific ambiences and effects upon the people who hear it. And [spiritual leader G. I.] Gurdjieff's objective music, some of which Keith Jarrett has recorded, was involved with some of these ideas. Color, tonal center correlations, vibrations that affect different organs of the body—all of this is quite fascinating, and it's also at the crux of what new age was originally about. That's what made new age stand out as a different category of music."

But Isham also feels that with these seeds, new age also sowed its own destruction. "I come back to the idea that music is a form of communication," he says. "It operates under basic laws of communication. Somebody has to intend to communicate, then move a message through time and space toward another person, and that other person has to duplicate the first person's intention in one way or another. Although it's easy to understand words and thoughts in this scheme, music as a communication operates at an even more powerful level than words. I mean, who was Verdi's librettist? Who was Mozart's librettist? Nobody remembers. But you remember those operas, boy! You remember that music. That's where art operates. The potential in that operating waveband is what interests me. And because a lot of the original new age music turned its back on Western, and even Eastern, traditions of sophistication, virtuosity, playing in tune, playing in time—the basic things that we've all come to accept as being indicators of good use of music, it left me cold from the start."

Along that line, Isham feels that adult contemporary music—new age in uptown dress—may have a negative impact on the art of music. "We live in experimental times," he muses. "This idea of stripping things down, of finding a simple sound, is a dangerous game. Now, I appreciate simplicity too. I think that you can have

simplicity as well as depth. But I can at times become unpleasantly arrogant about the naiveté and lack of sophistication in a lot of music. In any field of endeavor, there's a scale of excellence. I just wonder whether the public view of music is uneducated to the point that this scale of excellence is not understood."

* * * *

Synthesizers are a relatively recent addition to the list of instruments that you play. Have your trumpet chops influenced your synthesizer techniques?

Because I've played trumpet, my understanding of synthesizer performance comes from a traditional background: I'm quite aware of more than just the notes of a work. Basically, phrasing characterizes the sound of a "real" instrument as opposed to a so-called "synthetic" instrument. But even when I find a sound on a synthesizer that works, in order to make it musical requires more than just phrasing. The way that you rhythmically place the notes is also very important. For instance, if you want to give the impression of a wind-generated sound, make sure that you stop the sound where you would breathe. Psychologically, the impression becomes synthetic if you play eight bars without a breath. By letting the sound breathe at the right spots, you give the sound a more real aspect. Nuances like that are more important to me than getting into a lot of [modulation] wheel or pitch-bending.

That seems like a Zawinul-influenced approach to synthesizer playing.

Yes, and as a matter of fact, I would say one of the things that I've always loved about his approach is that he never got hung up with a lot of expression devices, like wheels and levers. Yet, he gets more expression out of a synthesizer than most other people who play one.

He also played traditional instruments, including the violin, before taking up synthesizers.

My musical philosophy is similar to his. I think in that way, being a trumpet player has helped and influenced my synthesizer performance. Another aspect of what psychologically creates a good "natural" sound is ambience. If you play a trumpet in a very dead studio, the air still moves from the bell to the microphone. Even though there's no reverb and the room is dead, there is still air and time. When you plug a synthesizer directly into the desk [mixing board], there is no air or time. So, in order to get any sort of psychological realism in that sound, you have to supply those elements. You can supply air and time by going through an amp that's miked; but the easiest way is to add some time modulation. I never hook up a synthesizer without putting some delay on it to give it space. And I'll use any and everything; from a ten-minute decay on a Lexicon 224X with nothing but echo, all the way to a [Fender] Twin Reverb in a garage with a microphone on it—whatever space it needs to make sense. In fact, I would list delay lines as being as important as any instrument I use right now. As a matter of fact, they're probably the biggest influence that electronics have had on my trumpet playing.

Other than your trumpets, what instruments do you have?

I own an old Moog Modular 12, and ARP 2600, an Oberheim Four-Voice, a [Sequential] Prophet-5 with a Poly Sequencer, and Steiner EVI [Electronic Valve Instrument], a Roland MC4 and MC8 [MicroComposer sequencers], and a [Roland] Drumatix. I've also got a lot of odd bits and pieces, like ring modulators, frequency dividers, an MXR delay, an MXR pitch transposer, and a Lexicon Prime Time II.

Have you modified any of this gear?

Yes, I have. My Prophet has been MIDIfied, but I'm not actually using that feature yet. The Four-Voice has been rebuilt with the keyboard separate from the rack-mounted voice modules, and there's a patch bay set up for all the internal points.

Have you MIDIed the Four-Voice through the patch bay?

No, I haven't. I've got a multi-pin connector that has control voltage and gates for all the voices and the master filter control. Everything that goes from the keyboard to the voices in the standard Four-Voice setup is also on a multi-pin connector that goes from the keyboard to the MicroComposer. So the system is composed of three parts—the rack of four voices, the keyboard, and the Micro-Composer—which are all connected by two multi-pin cords. In addition, there's a master clock channel which drives the Poly Sequencer; however, it's not the actual sync clock out of the MC4. It's one of the multiplex outputs which I've assigned to control the Poly Sequencer, which allows me to vary the clock rate, depending on the piece, of course.

Do you prefer the Oberheim's independently addressable voices to the Prophet's homophonic design?

I like having both. I certainly wouldn't give up the Prophet. I must admit that when I bought the Prophet two or three years ago it was against my better judgment. Sequential hadn't built the sequencer yet, and I've always refused to get involved with an instrument that wasn't expandable. But I needed something quick and programmable, and it's great for live performance. And when I did

the Walt Disney movie, *Never Cry Wolf*, it was the only thing I had with me.

How did you get involved with the film?

I had flown over from England to do the Rubisa Patrol reunion concert with Art Lande, so I only brought my trumpet, the Prophet, and the Poly Sequencer with me. Previously, I had recorded three demo tracks of synthesizer and bamboo flute music with Billy Douglass, who had played all the bamboo flute stuff for *The Black Stallion*. He had taken a copy of the demo tape to David Grove, who was doing the poster art for *Never Cry Wolf* and had also done the poster for *The Black Stallion*. Anyway, Carroll [Ballard, director for *Never Cry Wolf*] heard the demo tape because of David and asked who the synthesizer player was. As a result, I was asked to a screening of the film at Fantasy Studios along with several other film composers. I really had no intention of trying to make a bid on the project, since I was only going to be in the country for four or five days to do the one concert. A couple of days later, the line producer, Walker Stuart, phoned me and said that the director really wanted to meet me. After we talked, he let me use an 8-track studio for two days to record four cues. After I played the tape for him, he thought about it for two days and then handed me the project, so I ended up staying five months. It's interesting, because I ended up using some of the basic ideas from those two days as themes for the movie.

And you used the Prophet for the entire soundtrack?

I used the Prophet 95% of the time, although I did end up renting an Oberheim Two-Voice near the end for a couple of sounds that I couldn't get on the Prophet. I must say that I learned more about the Prophet in the first month of scoring that movie than I would have otherwise. It's remarkable what it can really do if you push the instrument and yourself. Of course, Ballard pushed me too. He wasn't satisfied with just something that worked and was good. He wanted it just right, and he brought out the best in me.

Did he suggest certain sounds or leave it entirely up to you and then refine your inspirations?

He would play a videotape of the cue and talk through it: "Well, we're right here and we should get this sort of feeling and it should move to here. By this time it's got to be out." I'd take notes and then reach for the Prophet. While I watched the video, I'd play shapes, little themes, or melodic ideas and put them into separate banks of the sequencer. Then when I replayed the video, I could throw in the sequence program one or go immediately to program six, or play a big chord. In this way, I could be watching and throwing musical ideas together at the same time, just to see if they worked. The tape machine was always on and we'd always try to have the sound just right, so that if the music worked, we would be sure to have it down right then and there.

Are many of your compositions based on visual inspirations?

I always start with a sound. I either write from a new sound on the synthesizer or from the sound of the piano.

Were you aiming for that Windham Hill sound when you recorded your solo album for them?

Basically, yes; I mean, there was very little point in making a record for Windham Hill that wasn't going to satisfy them. I could have made a punk album and handed it to them, but it wouldn't have done anything, and it would have been a waste of everyone's time. There's definitely something in my musical personality that is very satisfied and happy with the writing style that fits them. I think [producer/engineer] Steve Miller knew that. I gave him a lot of demo tapes—things I'd been doing at home and old ideas that I had no use for in Group 87. And going through all the old things inspired me to write some new stuff. He went through it all and, knowing the label better than I, picked what he thought would work. I was quite surprised, actually, because I thought some of the things he selected would be a little bit too much.

How do you use your keyboard instruments?

They all have completely different personalities, and I'm not quite sure how to describe them. The Moog has a bottom end that I think is better than any other instrument. It can't always get the 'crack' you need with all that weight, so I'll use the ARP with it. A lot of the bass things I do are a combination of the two. Or if it doesn't need to be quite so heavy, just the ARP will do. There's something about those ARP filters that adds a real bite to the sound. But nothing beats the Moog for weight or for just completely outlandish effects. The one I have has no real attenuators on all the inputs. I only have one attenuator, so if I modulate something, it's either 100% or nothing—you can go nuts very quickly. I did a soundtrack for a theater piece in London where I forced myself to use just the Moog. After my experience with the Prophet, I feel that's a great way to get to know your instrument. Percussion sounds are great on the Oberheim. You can have a choir of marimba players going on. The 12dB per octave filters can be very buzzy though, so I'll go to the Prophet for a real smooth sound. I also used a PPG on the album. I don't own this instrument, but it has some nice sounds. It's one of the first ones, a PPG 2, and it seemed a bit clumsy, but I wasn't used to seeing just one parameter at a time.

There was also some acoustic piano playing on Vapor

Drawings. *Do you play the piano much?*

At different points in my life I have been quite comfortable playing the piano and have actually accepted work as a pianist. I've spent periods practicing a lot and enjoying the piano, but I've never studied it to the extent that I have the trumpet. I consider myself a reasonably decent trumpet player, but I know because of that I will never be a reasonably decent piano player. I've also been spoiled working with Art Lande: He's a real piano player. And as I mentioned earlier, I love to write at the piano.

With your experience playing the piano, can you load the MicroComposer and the Poly Sequencer by playing, rather than inputting each note in single-step mode?

It's much quicker for me to single-step. I'm very picky about accurate time, and I hate it when I try to play something rhythmically perfect and my fingers just don't respond. But once in a while, when I psych myself up, I can do it. Obviously, there are a great many things I can't play on the keyboards, so I micro-compose them one step at a time, especially for the Oberheim. The Oberheim keyboard is not very sophisticated in terms of voice assignment, so if I really want to keep the counterpoint clear and keep track of each voice, I use the Micro-Composer. For instance, "Raffles in Rio" is all micro-composed, except for the flute solo.

Do you notate your music before inputting it?

I always write out a bar chart. Roland gives you sheets for the MC4, which use rows and rows of numbers, but I do it from a musical standpoint. I've gotten quite quick about it, and I'm at the point where the notes are numbers for me. But I have to keep a bar chart, because if I deleted anything, I wouldn't know where I was in the tune.

Some of your sequenced compositions remind me of Tangerine Dream.

In terms of that type of writing, I'm much more influenced by Brian Eno and Steve Reich. As a matter of fact, I love random composition. I'll set up a rhythm to play with, then turn down the clock on the sequencer to a very slow rate, and play a whole bunch of notes. The clock only picks out certain arbitrary ones, and I go back and edit them in single-step mode. It's a way of finding interesting things. I'll use all the technology I can to discover something new. I'm thinking of having SMS [Small Modular Systems in San Francisco] custom-build a random composition instrument for me. It would be a complete sample-and-hold synthesizer, basically just a rack of four sample-and-hold circuits and a rack of random rhythm generators. Add to that a couple of analog sequencers that you can gate for a completely random composition and you could generate an infinite number of new ideas with random rhythms and notes. There's another way of doing it with the MicroComposer. It has to quantize what it sees at the voltage in, so I'd run a random series of notes out of the ARP into the MicroComposer, put the MC4 into record, and let it quantize the notes, then chop up sections of it and loop it. The point of all this is that I'm trying with all the gear I've got to find different ways of using random ideas; using technology to help generate musical ideas.

Isn't that a substitute for bouncing ideas off of other musicians?

Perhaps, but you'd have to find a very extraordinary person, or a wide variety of extraordinary people, to keep getting that kind of input.

Do you ever use your horns to control the other

instruments in your equipment setup?

Usually I just use the EVI as a controller for the ARP, because the actual EVI synthesizer itself is just too difficult to use in performance. Then again, the reason might be that they both use minijacks, and the ARP has many patching points. The only other instrument that I could use it with would be the Moog; the Oberheim's hard to interface with and the Prophet's almost impossible. But as I said before, I consider effects devices especially delays, as instruments. I'm very much into Phil Glass, Terry Riley, and Steve Reich, and I put delays on acoustic instruments in order to get an ensemble sound from a single instrument. If there's a piano available when we do a live gig, I run the piano, the trumpet mike, and the Steiner [EVI] through the main looping rack, which has the MXR Digital Delay, MXR Pitch Transposer, and Lexicon Prime Time II with the extended memory. At the New Performance Gallery [San Francisco] there was a beautiful piano so I miked it and made loops with just trumpet, piano and Steiner.

In the current Group 87 you have another synthesist in the band. What's his function?

That's Colin Chin. He plays all the bass lines on an Oberheim module and fills out the orchestrations on a [Yamaha] DX7 and a [Roland] Juno 60 when I play lead. In "The Mask Maker" [from *A Career In Dada Processing*] he plays all the keyboards because I'm on trumpet. Obviously, on the tunes where I play trumpet, he plays most of the keyboard stuff, although he doesn't have any sequences.

What kind of problems do you and the rest of the band encounter in trying to play along with all of your sequenced lines?

It's pretty easy. I run a separate, totally unaffected line directly out of the drum machine to our drummer, Brian MacLeod, and he runs it right into his mixer. So even if the power in the house goes down or the monitor guy falls asleep and pulls all of his faders down, he's still connected to me. And I must say that Brian has an incredible sense of how to play along with machines; he's brilliant at it. And of course, as long as he's with it, then everybody just plays along with him. The music can float a little bit on top of it all, but it basically seems to work fine. It has to, because with the MC4 you can't get into the program interactively. If something screws up, you have to count the bars and know where you are. If you're two bars behind, the program goes on without you.

Are you currently experimenting with more interactive setups?

Some of the newer compositions have been written

around an entirely different approach. The composition is written as four channels of things that repeat over and over. By performing with the faders and using echo you can make the system more interactive. I've also modified my Poly Sequencer. Paul Rutigliano at Sequential rewrote some of the software for the sequencer so that while a sequence is playing, you can hit another sequence button, and it finishes the current one before going on to the new one, all without dropping a beat. Now I can really interact with the system and change sequences in real time without having to hit buttons precisely in rhythm. The form of the piece opens wider because you can loop indefinitely right where you are and then move on when you're ready. I also program the MC4 to change the sound of the Four-Voice as well as the pitches, and to transpose the different lines, which I can also do directly from the keyboard. All of these things add up to a really exciting, interactive system that I can improvise with.

How would you characterize the sound of Group 87?

We're an instrumental band. We're what you would normally expect to be a fusion band, but for people who spent most of their lives learning how to solo and play crossover jazz music, we have none of the self-indulgent qualities that fusion groups tend to have, like setting up an intricate groove and seeing how intricate of a solo one of us can put on top. I think there are only two solos on the whole album [*A Career In Dada Processing*], and they're both eight bars long. The concept for our band was to explore textural composition. Using a lot of ideas that are very removed from fusion, jazz, or rock, and without any vocals, really separated our sound from the rest of the so-called modern era bands. I think that's why we're unique.

For all of your "modernness," you get away with more interesting chord progressions than most other techno-pop-jazz-cross-over bands. Can you explain that?

Again, I find that a lot of the fusion-type groups are self-indulgent in the way they discover a new voicing and run the tune though the most intricate chords without caring whether or not it really makes sense—intellectual intricacy for its own sake. The point is that all of us in the band have studied that kind of music and have played with a lot of those people. We have a lot of respect for the great players and great elements of that style. And when it's right for us to do some of that stuff, it's in our musical vocabulary. But we're also not afraid to use just a major triad. Most fusion bands will always use the most complex chord voicing they can think of. Our philosophy is that if it needs *C-E-G*, that's what it gets. If nothing else, that concept is what's going on in everybody's head. Which, in some ways, is more modern sounding and almost totally electronic, and in other ways it's much more acoustic. This band is a total blend of the two. It's hard to tell if we're electric or acoustic. We're never synthetic electronic because that's not our style, and yet we're still very warm-sounding, even with a lot of synthesizers.

You're also using a Buchla 406, aren't you?

Yeah, that's something brand new. The instrument belongs to Todd Boekelheide, who was the music editor for *Never Cry Wolf*. It was one of the first ones that Don [Buchla] made. Don's got a new [computer] language for it called CHOPS, which is oriented toward keyboard players, as opposed to his previous languages, MIDAS and PATCH. MIDAS is directed toward home composition, utilizing a more standard musical notation, whereas PATCH is a completely nontraditional language which is open to anything you want to do. With CHOPS you still have complete tuning control over every key on the keyboard. You can even assign a different sound to each key and split the keyboard anyway you want; it's completely open-ended. It's got a built-in sequencer, which he plans to expand. I've been working with Buchla to help find all the bugs, and I've gotten to the point where I have a few things programmed into it that I use in the show. I simply borrow Todd's instrument and bring my own floppy disks. But it's still not the complete answer for me. I need something that I can interact with in real time, and the only way I can see how to do that is the modular system I've got now.

Are you planning to change your setup?

Equipment-wise, I'm planning to change *everything*. I'm still looking for something like the Fairlight or the PPG 2.3, but I'm not convinced that either one of them is right. If I had $11,000 to throw at just a digital synthesizer, I'd probably buy Buchla's. I may buy a DX7 out of frustration; that would give me a MIDI keyboard with touch sensitivity, which the Prophet-5 doesn't have. I'm also incredibly interested in the [Oberheim] Xpander. My synthesizer background is analog, and that instrument could replace my old Four-Voice and be a lot more reliable. One of the problems with the Four-Voice is that there's no matrix between the control voltage and gate inputs and outputs, so the keyboard always affects the MicroComposer and vice-versa. I did that on purpose in order to keep the interactive capability high, but it's a pain for live performance. You have to remember to manually re-transpose everything when you go back and forth between keyboard and MicroComposer control of the voice modules. With the Xpander, I can program all that, which would obviously be a big help. And then with the

DX7 I can have a MIDI keyboard controller with a digital synthesizer built-in. Through the Prophet's MIDI I could drive the Poly Sequencer from the DX7, and going the other way, the DX7 could control the Xpander and the Prophet. The MC4 could also run the Xpander. That kind of system would be more flexible than what I have now, with a lot less hassle.

What are your plans musically?

I'm in the middle of another film, called *Mrs. Soffel*, which stars Diane Keaton and Mel Gibson. It's a Gillian Armstrong movie; she did *My Brilliant Career*. This is an interesting film and quite a challenge for me. It's not like anything I've ever done before.

How, if at all, does your commitment to the film affect Group 87?

Well, because of the movie, Group 87 is kind of on hold. We're also going through an identity crisis as a band—what to do. As it stands now, the band is with a major label [Capitol Records] and they don't understand what we're doing. We get pissed off when they don't do anything, they don't know what to do, and we don't have the type of management that understands how to manipulate the record company to do what should be done. So if we manage to hang on to our major record deal we're coming up with a plan that will hopefully give them a product that they will understand. We won't be selling out musically, but we'll be looking for the common ground; something that we do that they know how to sell. The way it's going, it's not good for them or us.

What kind of an album would it be?

It will probably be in the realm of a dance record; something with a groove that just won't quit, but that still has us on top of it. We don't want to alienate anybody. And I think that's well within our direction as Group 87. Look at "Rockit" by Herbie Hancock—it can be done. But I think we'd do it in a little more dignified way than Herbie's been doing it over the past couple of years. He's so obvious. He has one concession to commercialism on an album and then just blows free for the rest of the tracks.

How would you do it differently?

We would really try to conceptually come up with an identity that is in fact Group 87, but that would really work for the record company. And we'd really stick to it, and not just treat it as a concession. We would treat it as a challenge to make it work for us and for them. It might mean doing half a record as a dance side and the other half as the ambience side, or do the entire thing as a dance record, like [producer/bassist] Trevor Horn's *Art Of Noise* album. That would be a crossover point for us. Also, our percussionist, Ron [MacLeod], has really influenced the sound of our band. There might be another alternative, which would be to forget the major labels and concentrate on the alternative music scene. Peter Baumann has a new label called Private Music that we're checking out, among others. But regardless of our label, the structure of the band is going to have to change. It can't really come down to me and Peter.

You mean the others are going to have to contribute more to the band in terms of musical direction?

It's going to have to be a slightly more directed focal point. I've got too much other stuff going on to be involved 100 percent of the time. And since the beginning, there's been a weakness on our part from the business point of view. We need a real directed business side. Unless this problem can be solved, the band is going to have some problems. So it's a real transition period for the band right now.

Personally, what's your focal point now?

The solo stuff feels great, and Windham Hill has been really responsive. They managed to sell more albums than the two Group 87 records combined. They want to do a second album and are interested in releasing the soundtrack for the new film when the movie comes out. And I've got an agent in Hollywood who seems to think he can keep me employed as a film writer, so those things look pretty good. So I'm focusing on three specific areas: Windham Hill, Group 87, and films. ☐

A Selected Mark Ishham Discography
Solo albums: *Castalia*, Virgin, 90900-4. (On Windham Hill): *Vapor Drawings*, 1027; *Film Music*, 1041. **With Group 87:** *A Career In Dada Processing*, Capitol, ST-12334; *Group 87*, Columbia, JC-36338, out of print. **With Van Morrison** (on Warner Bros.): *Beautiful Vision*, BSK-3652; *Common One*, BSK-3462; *Inarticulate Speech Of The Heart*, 1-23802, *Into The Music*, HS-3390. **With Will Ackerman:** *Past Light*, Windham Hill, WH-1028.

KITARO

By Freff

A study in contrasts: On the screen, a slender oriental man of fierce demeanor pounds savagely against a giant Japanese drum. The drum is at least twice his size. The drumsticks are cudgels. The thunder is enormous, the rhythm totally absorbing. If you look close, past the flapping kimono sleeves, you can see that his fists have been taped closed over the drumsticks, the fingers of his hands long since exhausted past any capacity to hold on.

Beside me the same man, wearing a blue jogging suit is in the process of doing in several slices of a typically greasy New York pizza.

This is Kitaro? Enigmatic Japanese synthesist, cultural hero, reputed hermit?

Well, yeah.

Keyboard, May 1986

Back to the screen: It's fireworks time now, and Kitaro has become a living dragon. Held tight to his side is a bamboo cylinder about four feet long that has been wrapped in thick rope. The cylinder's opening is right next to his head, and from that opening a column of fire spouts 30 feet or more into the glow of approaching dawn. The camera moves in for a closeup of Kitaro's face, serene and stoic against a pyrotechnic torrent of windblown sparks.

Beside me the same man has finished the pizza and is now draining a liter of Coca-Cola.

This, I think to myself, is going to be interesting.

Nearly all of Kitaro's albums begin with the sound of water. Sometimes crashing ocean waves, sometimes gently running streams, sometimes the hushed susurrus of rain in forest trees—but again and again, water: changeless in the broad perspective, constantly changing when examined closely. That's not a bad metaphor for Kitaro's music itself. With at least a dozen albums and soundtracks to his name, he has created a body of recorded music that has been wildly successful while completely defying all corporate standards of what is "commercial." People who don't like it will tell you it all sounds the same, that it is remarkably naive, that it neither rocks nor swings and has no energy. People who do like it (and they are legion, especially outside the States; Kitaro is one of the biggest concert draws ever in Asia, the *only* man to play both Taiwan and Communist China) will tell you that it has plenty of energy, but energy of a different kind, and that it moves steadily, as nature does, in a constant passage from one state to the next. They treasure exactly the naivete that Kitaro's detractors hate, and ask what kind of cynic it takes to dislike the musical equivalent of sunrises and thunderstorms.

It may be true that one Kitaro album sounds a lot like another—but is this such a bad thing? After all, Kitaro is *shooting* for timelessness. He is deliberately straddling cultures, collecting magpie pieces of this and that. He aims to transport his listeners beyond the things that bind them—and he succeeds.

What makes the music work, naive or not, is that Kitaro is sincere. His music matches his spirit, and he has come by both quite naturally.

Born in Central Japan in 1953 to a family of Buddhist/Shintoist farmers, he was raised in comparative isolation and an atmosphere of calm. Forget your Western images of the farmer as agribusinessman—most of the corn, rice, radishes, and spinach his family grew was for their own consumption, not for market. Music didn't figure into Kitaro's life at all until he was a senior in high school. There, at least, he did things in a way most of us will be familiar with: He picked up an electric guitar, learned it by ear, and played R&B and Beatles covers in a seemingly endless string of bands. But he had switched over to keyboards by the time he started recording albums with the Far East Family Band in the early '70s; and it is keyboard work that has been the basis not only of his music's development, but also its success.

While in England with the Far East Family Band Kitaro met Klaus Schulze, who showed him there was more to synthesizers than he had previously considered. The explorations that that meeting inspired eventually found their way onto his first and second solo records, *Astral Voyager* (this is Kitaro's title; the Geffen catalog lists it as *Astral Voyage*) and *Full Moon Story*, which established him as Japan's premier pop synthesist in much the way that Keith Emerson dominated Europe during the same period.

Kitaro's big break came with *Silk Road*, a documentary soundtrack job for Japan's national television network, NHK. This one-shot, about the overland trade route from Europe to Japan proved so popular that it spawned a series that ran for five years and made Kitaro a star. And not just in Japan, either, but all over Asia, and then Europe as his albums were released there, and even—in an underground way—in the States, when his European and Japanese releases hit the import lists. The most recent sign that Kitaro is onto something is that Geffen Records (not a company known for their championing of unlikely causes) signed him to a worldwide deal in early 1986. They put out one blitzkrieg release of seven albums in midsummer, and now they've released *Tenku*, his newest and the first recorded specifically for Geffen.

The career and the music are a lot easier to describe than the man.

Partially it is the contrasts: Westerners prefer to deal with contradiction by ignoring one thing or the other, not by adopting both wholeheartedly. Kitaro, on the other hand, works with both the highest and lowest of technology in his recording. He tracks a Kurzweil 250 against obscure ethnic hand instruments acquired in his travels. He records in a very well-equipped private studio, but since it happens to be in his home in the Japanese Alps he typically throws open the window and lets the trees and birds cut their own backing tracks. He beats ceremonial drums until his hands are bloody, then wanders around the meadows of his farm passing and punting a football. (Direct quote, and we're not kidding: "It's unbelievable how far American quarterbacks can throw the ball!" This from a man who recently threw a private concert, in a cave with some considerable religious significance, where his music was strictly backup to a series of traditional Japanese floral arrangements!)

No, it's not a small world. It's a very, very large world. But it certainly folds together in funny places.

* * * *

You didn't start making music until you were 18, and then what you got into was electric guitar. It's quite a distance from "Dock Of The Bay" and "Day Tripper" to what you're doing now.

Yes, it is a long way. When I started in music I formed and played in a typical cover band. But around the time I was 19 I wrote my first original tune. It wasn't rock and roll, or anything in particular, just a song. I composed it on my guitar. I liked composing, so I wrote more songs, and played them in various groups I formed in the following years. I don't know that there was any dramatic change in my personal life that was responsible for the changes in my music. It was, rather, a natural sort of transition. Playing in bands was good, but keeping these groups together was a difficult task. I learned other instruments out of necessity. One of my group members was killed in a traffic accident, so I had to learn to play keyboards. When my bass player got sick, I had to learn to play bass. The same was true for drums. But of all of them I was drawn to the keyboard rather strongly, and that was the start of my present course in music.

When I finally tired of dealing with groups, I decided to go solo: I was in my early 20s, I was thinking more seriously about my own music, and it was just natural that I would eventually want to go it on my own. It was something of a challenge to see if I could do it by myself. That was *Astral Voyager* [1978], the first product of my combining my desire to compose with deep personal thought. Then I landed the NHK television documentary project, *Silk Road*, and the rest has just been a natural progression. I've been composing and recording solo works ever since.

You are very prolific.

Yes, that's true. In 1980 alone I recorded four albums. When I compose a piece, I start with a mental picture—a painting, really. For me there is always a sound associated with that mental image. So when I sit down at my instruments and recording gear, I already have the sound in my head. It's a process of laying down the tracks to re-create the music in my mind. As I record, of course, I will modify and embellish the sound as I see fit. With the new album, *Tenku*, I wanted to create something that was like a childhood dream; when I started, that was my overall theme. I tried to recall the dreams and fantasies I had as a child, and each track represents one of those fantasies—like sprouting wings and flying away to some far place, or crossing the boundaries of time.

I "played" in the music much as a child would play in his fantasies, devoting three months to bringing these images together. It wasn't three months of constant work, but a period in which I'd put in several days at a time—typically ten days—of heavily concentrated effort. When I work, I barely sleep or eat. But then I rest to regain my energy. Each of the "dreams" in *Tenku* represents many hours of composition and recording in this fashion. But together, the pieces are one work. I like to think of each of my albums as whole work, with the individual tracks like movements in a classical composition.

Let's talk tools.

As you know, I use a combination of synthesized and acoustic sounds. I like my synthesizers, and I like my acoustic instruments. I also like and use natural sounds.

But what about your actual working relationship with your tools? What do you think, for example, about your Yamaha DX7 as opposed to your Kurzweil 250 as opposed to your piano as opposed to your traditional Japanese drum?

You mentioned the DX7. It's an impressive instrument. It can produce a wide range of sounds—some of them quite natural—and it does it all rather inexpensively. I do feel it lacks a certain warmth, but I like the instrument. And the Yamaha people are very helpful. I can go to the Yamaha factory with specific requests for modifying certain sounds, and they'll work with me to get the instrument to produce the sound I want. I also like my Kurzweil, not only because it lets me do sampling, but also because it has a wide range of tonal capabilities and its sound quality is generally excellent. Of course, it's expensive—but it's worth it. I use the Kurzweil quite a bit in my recording. That company, too, has been very cooperative in helping me get what I want out of the instrument. I think they make a great product, though one that is difficult to master. The Kurzweil importer in Japan provided me only with the original English manual. I had to have a friend translate the whole thing for me, and even with that I found the Kurzweil difficult. Using the instrument's display to create sounds involves a heavy mental conversion process. I've started to use the Macintosh computer to program the instrument, and that helps. But it's still not an easy instrument to use.

I guess my most pronounced preference is still for analog synthesizers—for example, the Minimoog. I like analog synthesizers because I feel I can really create totally new sounds from scratch. Digital synthesizers, more often than not, force you to build with factory-programmed sounds. It's hard to describe, but I feel that analog synthesizers are better suited to my music because it is born of mental images. That's why I will continue to rely more heavily on these instruments than on the digital variety. In addition to the Minimoog I use the Roland Jupiter-8 and the Korg 700-800 DV (double voice).

Your position as a synthesizer player is certainly secure. But since you began recording, the synthesizer industry has completely changed, with your countrymen's products coming to dominate. How do you feel about this from your perspective as a Japanese synthesist?

I think the strength of the Japanese companies lies in their ability to bring tremendous technological and manufacturing know-how to bear on producing a large number of instruments with a tremendous range of capabilities for mass consumption. I feel that Japanese manufacturers are, by and large, making instruments that are almost toy-like—there's not real quality there. I'd like to tell these companies to turn their attention and capabilities toward producing really great, world-class instruments. If the quality is there, I don't mind paying for it. Forget about trying to cram the most features for the money into an instrument. Give me real quality. I have observed that a lot of Japanese equipment I use, for example, can't stand up to the rigors of concert use.

Those are strong words.

Well, I think all manufacturers are genuinely trying to make a good product and giving their designs a lot of thought. It's just that a lot of companies seem to lack a design policy—there's no attempt to create and maintain an identity, and their products often reflect a hasty reaction to what their competitors have done.

What about your acoustic instruments?

I own a Japanese drum—a large, old, expensive thing. It appeals to me because it is an instrument that has only one surface to strike, only one way to produce sound. But that's the beauty. Within that limitation is a wide tonal variety that can be produced. With just two sticks and one surface I can express a tremendous range of emotions very directly. I like to believe it lets me convey a lot of power—the musical and emotional power that is in me. I also play the conventional drum set, the harp, and other traditional Japanese instruments like the koto. And I'm an avid collector of native instruments from other countries. For example, I've played many Indian instruments on my recordings, such as the sitar and *santool*, and whenever I make foreign trips I return with lots of instruments. Interestingly, I tend to buy native acoustic instruments in Europe and Asia, but when I come to the U.S. I usually seek out new electronic instruments.

You are entirely self-taught. Has that helped or hurt you as a musician?

I've never liked the way they teach music in Japan, so, in that sense, I'm glad I didn't study music formally there. When it comes to playing instruments, my compositions have driven me: I've always taught myself to produce the sounds that I needed. Playing the harp, for instance, I practiced until I was satisfied that I could play the parts I wanted. A normally trained harpist might look at me and find fault with my technique, but I don't think that makes my playing less valid. What counts is that I have achieved the sound I set out to achieve for my music.

How is music taught in Japan?

My objection to the way music is taught in Japan is that it is too rigid in many ways. Typical teachers at Japanese music schools try too hard to make students fit a preconceived pattern. There is too much emphasis on technique and not enough on the music itself; there is no heart in their teaching.

Still, is there anything you wish you played better?

Yes, the violin. I've always used my synthesizers to produce string-like sounds. But I own a violin—a good one—and I want to be able to play it in my recordings. So I'm busy practicing now.

Can you explain what happens when an instrument—say, that violin—is just impossible to learn well enough, in a short enough time, for you to capture what's in your head? Doesn't that ever frustrate you? And what about the argument that being self-taught

leaves a musician with inadequate technique?

Certainly, I experience those frustrations. Sometimes I rely on technology to get around the problem. For example, if it's a matter of not being able to play a passage up to tempo, I can record it more slowly and then speed it up mechanically or electronically. But techniques like that are a last resort. I will always do everything I can first to play the passage, so I can record it in real time.

What about the use of sequencers?

I haven't used sequencers very much in my recordings thus far, but I can foresee using them more. They can help overcome deficiencies in instrumental technique, but I don't like using sequencers for repetitive phrases. Somehow it comes out sounding too mechanical. That's why I've always manually played my passages, wherever possible. As for MIDI, I haven't used MIDI for recording very much at all, though I am exploring using it to save me tracks on my tape recorder, thus expanding my capabilities. Where I *have* used MIDI sequencers is when I perform live, as in my latest Japanese concert tour, where I was using a Yamaha QX1 in combination with a TX816 rack and DX7 and DX5 keyboards.

Are you self-taught as a recording engineer, too?

My first multi-channel recording was made on an 8-track deck that I had personally modified to run at 30 ips. I've always had an interest in electronics, and did some studying on my own. When I needed to get more

performance out of my tape deck, I knew what I had to do. As far as recording technique goes, I picked that up as I went along. I learned by doing.

Your official bio says only, "Kitaro met Klaus Schulze and discovered the synthesizer." There must be more to the story than that!

I met Klaus at Manor Studios in Oxford. I was there recording an album with the Far East Family Band for Virgin Records, and Klaus was producing. On one of our days off he and I found ourselves together in an impromptu session. During that session I noticed Klaus using the synthesizer in what I thought were unusual ways. He was playing on *my* Minimoog and producing sounds I had never heard from that instrument. It made quite an impression on me. I realized then that there were some unique and different ways of using this instrument.

Was that sort of a personal quest?

Well, it *was* an inspiration. I remember it even today. What I learned was that there were ways to use the synthesizer well above and beyond the instructions in the owner's manual. The book essentially tells you which knobs to turn or buttons to push to get certain sounds. Klaus's approach was completely different. It's a matter of constantly searching within yourself for new, fresh ways to approach the instrument—to go beyond what the manufacturer says you can do.

How do you avoid repeating yourself?

You know, I never feel exactly the same way year to

year, month to month, or even day to day. I'm not the same person I was last year. I hope I am constantly growing. My music is always a reflection of where I am and who I am at the time I write it. With growth comes change. And so, in a sense, I don't think it's possible for me to do the same thing, the same way, twice.

Does the traveling you do contribute to that growth? You seem to take full advantage of the opportunities your music has provided you to see the world.

I've always traveled a lot, even before I traveled as a performing musician. Just meeting many people and hearing many different people and hearing many different instruments and sounds has had, I'm sure, a profound effect on my personal and professional growth. I'll never forget one time in India when I listened to an old blind man play the *santool.* I was mesmerized. I thought to myself, "Here's a one-man Tangerine Dream."

You're a prolific performer, as well as recording artist, but some of your performances aren't exactly club dates. I'm thinking of the video where you were on a hill at dawn, beating an immense traditional drum, which I gather is a regular annual ritual for you.

Although I now live just a bit farther away, I used to—up until about seven years ago—live right on Mt. Fuji. During that time I got some very strong feelings from the mountain; it was almost as if Mt. Fuji were looking after me, taking care of me. I wanted to show my appreciation to this guardian, so I devised this ceremony. I perform it every year on a full moon night in August. It's really a prayer of thanks to Mt. Fuji. I set my Japanese drum on the mountainside and play for about 11 hours. Straight. I only stop when I fall unconscious, which will happen several times during a night, and I resume playing as soon as I regain consciousness. Toward morning, I have to tape my fists closed over the drumsticks in order to continue. Over the past few years this ceremony has been spreading. Friends of mine in several locations around Japan have set up their own drums and begun the ritual at the same appointed hour. Last August, some American Indian friends of mine joined me in this ceremony. Perhaps, one day, it could be a worldwide event.

If it's that physically punishing, why do you do it?

I do it every year because of the gratitude I feel for the mountain. And that's really it. I don't think for a moment that by performing this ritual there will be some kind of reward later, in this life or after, or that some good will come to me because I do this. Nothing like that. Just gratitude. That's okay, isn't it?

It's fine. But it's tough to imagine an exact American equivalent. People here aren't generally willing to knock themselves out to that extent for so abstract a concept.

I will say this: performing this drum ceremony has put me in touch with a part of myself that I didn't know existed, a sense of "Wow, do I really have that kind of energy within me?" It's an incredible feeling to know you have that kind of strength within.

What about the fireworks in the event?

The town I grew up in happens to be famous for its fireworks. I became fascinated with fireworks and learned to make my own; in fact, I am now a licensed fireworks maker. I derive much of the same satisfaction and enjoyment from making fireworks that I do from recording my music. And it was my own fireworks that were used during the drum ceremony.

That's not something that you just pick up on a weekend. How did you get into this?

I just wanted to become licensed so that I could make and perform my own fireworks. So I read up on it and visited fireworks factories until I had learned enough to apply for my license. No special reason. I just wanted to do it. In the town where I was born there are certain varieties of fireworks that are seen only in that town. They are hand-held. Explosives are packed into a bamboo cylinder, which is then wrapped tightly with rope. The thing shoots sparks up about 20 meters into the air. And since you *hold* the cylinder next to you, the fireworks are erupting from the opening right next to your face. So, you do have to know what you're doing.

We're going to leap back to music.

Oh, yes. I remember now. I'm a musician.

Actually, I'm beginning to wonder whether you're a musician or something considerably different. You seem to be intent on living a life, a very specific life, and music is only one of the ways that that life is taking shape.

I'd agree with that. I don't really like to think of music as a profession. Of course, that's what it is, but for me it's considerably more than that.

What about more typical concerts? There's quite a contrast between your isolated composing and recording style and being in front of live crowds. What does performance give you that recording doesn't?

A composition or an album is a work of art, much as a novel or painting. When one records, one strives for perfection. Not that I don't strive for perfection in my live concerts, but it's not the same thing. At a concert I can react to the mood of the moment. If I really get into one piece, I can take it where I want, for as long as I want. Live performances communicate a certain kind of power that neither the performer nor listener can experience in recordings.

Given that you strive for perfection in your recordings, are there any you are more satisfied with than others for any reason?

Although I really do like all of the albums I've recorded so far, I feel particularly happy with *Tenku*, because of its theme, the evoking of childhood memories. You see, I have a son who just turned two years old. There's a child's voice on one of the tracks; that is him, and so the theme and the pieces have special meaning for me.

Tell us more.

Well, there's a lot going on in the individual tracks, and I wouldn't know where to start. But I can tell you this. I labored over the final mix for each of the tracks more than I ever did with my previous albums. The engineering for *Tenku* was much more involved, and also much more elaborate.

Why?

Much of my previous work was an outgrowth of the *Silk Road* project. Because it was an NHK television documentary series, the theme already existed, and I had to write to fit that theme. *Tenku* is something I created entirely on my own. Also, *Tenku* is the first album of mine that will enjoy immediate worldwide distribution through Geffen Records. I guess the combination of these things made me feel as though *Tenku* was something of a new beginning for me. I wanted to be absolutely sure of every detail on the album. So I double-checked, triple-checked, and so on. There's something else, too. In order to create *Tenku* I really returned to my own childhood. As children we have dreams, fantasies, aspirations. Not that we don't have these as adults, but somehow we were all at a purer, more elevated level of mind as children, before the world around us began to corrupt and pollute our thinking. Trying to return to this pure state of mind was not an easy task.

Do you feel your music is Japanese? To our ears there's a rather Western sound to a lot of it. In fact, much of it seems right in line with the Romantic tradition in Western music, as opposed to any sort of Japanese tradition or approach.

I like to think of my music as being universal rather than Japanese or Western. Each culture has its traditional music. When I think of Japanese music, I think

of—oh, for example, the music one hears in the Kabuki theater. My music isn't "Japanese" in that traditional sense any more than current American music is traditionally "American." Now, that's not to say that traditional Japanese music doesn't have any influence on my work. Having grown up in Japan, I can't help but be influenced by my country's traditions. But I think the people of my generation have grown up listening to music of many cultures; and because I grew up listening to a lot of Western music, I can't help but be influenced by traditional Western sounds. I think you'll hear both in my music. To have relevance to the current generation of listeners, I believe new music should have this universal quality.

Even with the Geffen PR push behind you, Japan is still far away. Are there other people like you that we haven't heard about? Are you all alone doing this thing, or do you represent a wave of people in Japan who think in a similar fashion?

I believe there are others like me in Japan. I read about them in magazines. But because I hardly ever listen to other people's music, I can't tell you what their music is like.

Do you listen to anyone's music now?

I listen to my own music quite a bit. Not just because I'm writing it, either. I find, for example, that listening to my music helps me sleep better at night.

Editor's Note: While Kitaro's English was certainly good enough for him to understand our questions, it wasn't up to answering them in a manner that matched the precision of his thoughts. So we had a kind of three-way conversation, with Kitaro and translator Herron Appleman carrying on at great length, and having what looked to be a wonderful time, in Japanese. Every now and then Herron would take pity on us, give us the Cliff Notes version of what had just been said, and we'd ask another question. Herron later provided us with a complete translation of the results. □

A Selected Kitaro Discography
Solo albums (on Geffen): *Asia*, GHS 24087; *Astral Voyage*, GHS 24082; *Full Moon Story*, GHS 24083; *India*, GHS 24085; *Millenia*, GHS 24084; *Silver Cloud*, GHS 24086; *Tenku*, GHS 24112; *Toward The West*, GHS 24094. *In Person*, Gravity (dist. by Gramavision), 18-7007-1; *Ki*, Kukuck Schallplatten (Habsburgerplatz 2, 8000 Munchen 40, West Germany), 0057; *Silk Road Suite* (London Symphony, 2-LP set), Kukuck Schallplatten, 065-066; *Tunhuang*, Kuckuck, Schallplatten, 058.

PATRICK O'HEARN

By Jeff Burger, Dominic Milano,
and Bob Doerschuk

Keyboard, January 1987
and September 1988

Really, you've been slaving over those old analog washers and dryers long enough. It's time you went down to Sears and picked up a pair of the new Kenmore digital laundry machines. Tell the salesperson you saw this great 32-track model—no, it's not in the catalog. This Mitsubishi 800 32-track digital recorder was in . . . Patrick O'Hearn's laundry room?

It was matters practical rather than musical that led this inspired new age synthesist to such an unusual setup. O'Hearn has just completed his second LP for Private Music, the electronic music label founded a few years ago by ex-Tangerine Dreamer Peter Baumann. His first album, *Ancient Dreams,* was a charter LP for the label—and not cheap. "One of the terms of agreement with Private Music is that everything must be recorded digitally, so you're talking about the most expensive format right now—$2,000 a day to record," O'Hearn explains. "That's outrageous unless you're mixing the next Madonna single. If you're looking at recording a rather esoteric instrumental record, it's suicide! When it came time to do the second record, I was having reservations about doing it digitally, because as a royalty artist, you're never going to be able to recoup the funds."

O'Hearn brought these concerns to Baumann, who had similar thoughts. Their economic solution: a package rental of a 32-track digital recorder and a custom-built 32-channel board, complete with short-term installation at O'Hearn's home in Simi Valley, California. After setting up the instruments and board, however, there was no room left for the 32-track machine. O'Hearn was therefore forced to run snakes down the hall to the only available space in the house—the laundry room. While he feels his engineering chops could stand improving, this method allowed him to experiment in directions that would not otherwise have been affordable. He has been forwarding rough mixes to the label, but the final tracks will be mixed professionally at a high-end studio sporting a good deal of processing gear.

In trying to engineer and perform simultaneously, O'Hearn found his Roland MC-500 sequencer invaluable. His tape sync scheme is a bit convoluted, but effective. O'Hearn first lays a quarter-note pattern on tape, with the MC-500 driving a cowbell sample on the Akai S900. He then retrieves that pattern with a Doctor Click, which sends a 48-ppq pulse to a JL Cooper MIDI Sync 1, converting the sync to MIDI clocks. A digital delay is inserted between the two devices to compensate for unwanted delays due to MIDI, or to change the feel. The MIDI clock is then mixed with incoming MIDI performance data via a JL Cooper MIDI Blender. O'Hearn favors Doctor Click, noting that "with the tape sync you always have to start at the top of the composition in order to engage the seqencer in sync. The Doctor Click is able to drop in one quarter-note before wherever it is you want to drop in."

O'Hearn does most of his initial recording on the sequencer one track at a time, edits if necessary, and then dumps that to tape before beginning the next track. He also stores the tracks to disk, so he can later replace the instrumentation while retaining the performance. To build sound layers, he usually uses a combination of Akai S900, Oberheim Xpander—which he cites for its diverse sound palette ranging from "lush and gentle" to "very exotic"—and his favorite keyboard, a MIDIed PPG Wave 2.2. "For anything with the hard transients, I look to the ARP 2600 or Oberheim modular stuff," he explains. "The PPG is capable of generating very warm sounds, as well as very harsh and annoying types of sounds. Even though I've had the PPG for about five years now, I still stumble onto certain areas that really are exciting."

In his sampling, O'Hearn veers toward the unusual. "Sampling for me is really wonderful for developing percussion sounds from unorthodox types of instruments—cutting and pasting different textures together that have never been heard before." He takes a 2-track recorder out in his travels to capture sounds like beat-

ing on a garage door, door springs, or a car. "I have what would seem like the world's largest concert drum," he says, laughing, "which is in fact an old beat-up Maytag dryer door hit with a rubber mallet!" More digital laundry.

Patrick O'Hearn has paid his musical dues for at least 15 years, but mostly as a bass player. From his first

gig as a nine-year-old playing standards in his parents' nightclub act, he eventually wound up on acoustic bass behind such jazz heavyweights as saxophonists Dexter Gordon, Joe Henderson, and Charles Lloyd and guitarist Joe Pass. Losing out to Stanley Clarke when Chick Corea's band made the acoustic-to-electric transition, O'Hearn dusted off his electric bass and played "Barnum and Bailey, no-holds-barred rock and roll" in Frank Zappa's group for three years. After a stint with the ill-fated but seminal Group 87, O'Hearn cut a demo with Missing Persons and spent a year or two in Tony Williams' Lifetime while Missing Persons flogged tapes in search of a contract. Patrick O'Hearn rejoined and stayed with Missing Persons until their demise in August 1986.

The years with Zappa stimulated O'Hearn's interest in keyboards. "Frank always had a ravenous appetite for the latest technological gadgetry that was out on the market," he says. "In 1976 he bought this immense E-mu modular system that would take a Bekins moving van to move—the thing was just mind-boggling to look at." That, he claims, was what did it. In 1979 he bought his first synth, a Micromoog, and has continued to collect favorite machines ever since. "When I joined Missing Persons, they wanted synthesized bass, so I wound up playing Minimoog in concert. That's really when I started playing keyboard. I'd also play occasional pads on other instruments to help fortify the arrangements."

O'Hearn doesn't see himself as a master keyboardist; for him, the keyboard is mainly a good controller. But not always the ideal controller, he cautions. "I was up at Zappa's house the other night, and he was playing back these wild classical avant-garde pieces. He said he had entered everything in on the Roland Octapad. He said it was the only thing fast enough to do the job! Some of the rolls, flams, and feels were done in a way that would be physically impossible to do on a keyboard."

While he doesn't categorize his electronic music work as definitive new age, O'Hearn sees a positive trend in that area, fueled largely by baby boomers dissatisfied with the modern airwaves. For new age performers, he observes, "Avenues are springing up like wildfire. There's a new age-genre label popping up every day; I think a lot of people are going to have the opportunity to have their tapes listened to. New age predominantly seems to be electroncially based. Two years ago it was new wave, now it's new age."

"Roland has made such tremendous improvement in their on-board patches these past few years," O'Hearn continues. "The factory patches used to be the laughing stock of their instruments; they'd say 'bassoon' or 'oboe,' but sound like a kazoo. But that's changed. The D-50 has got some killer sounds. Unfortunately, it is a little noisy. That's fine for live work, but if you're going for a real subtle string pad or a low sustain pad in the studio, you'll really hear it if it's exposed. That's why I usually give it a subordinate role. Even so, a friend of mine called me after hearing *Rivers Gonna Rise* on CD and said, 'What's the deal here? I thought this was a digital recording. We're going to deduct ten points for the noise!'"

Though O'Hearn admits to mixed feelings about sampling, he uses his Akai S900 extensively, especially for percussion. "It's mainly a rhythm instrument," he insists. "I don't use it much at all for polyphony. As a late bloomer in the personal computer world, I recently picked up on Digidesign's Softsynth, which is a delightful program. I was mainly knocked out about its additive possibilities. In order to play those sounds back, they have to be shovelled over to the S900, so it's now coming forward as a melody instrument for me too, with chords and everything.

"I have a problem with sampling in general, though. It seems to work very well on certain types of things. I haven't analyzed what works, what doesn't, and why, but I will do that soon because I really do love the S900. It gives a lot for the price, although it is difficult for me to sample things off of some disks. I bought Terry Fryer's Earworks Volume I disk, which has some beautiful pecussion samples, but it's very hard to get them across to the S900."

As a relative newcomer to PCs, O'Hearn is finally getting ready to set his Roland MC-500 on the shelf and move into software sequencing. "The MC-500 has been wonderful," he says. "But it's difficult to work in that you've only got the given four open tracks at one time, so you've got to bounce and merge and extract. It's so much less of a headache when you are working with a personal computer."

But which one lies in O'Hearns's future? "I was looking at the Atari," he says, "but then I went to the Mac Music Festival at Paramount Studios last November, and I was quite impressed by the amount of software and support going on for the Macintosh. Though other computer manufacturers wouldn't want to admit it, the Mac seems to be the industry standard."

The big enchilada in O'Hearn's studio is his huge Harrison board, bought used from a studio in Nashville. He has on occasion used all 32 tracks on the Mitsubishi 32-track digital recorder he rents for all his sessions, "but only because we got very liberal with recording stereo pairs," he notes. "Given the extra channels, you can do things like print weird reverbs or delays, or, on a MIDIed setup where you're going to meld two or three instruments to a discrete stereo pair, isolate them and have their balances addressed separately until the time comes to bounce them together. It was probably a little excessive, but recording 32-track is a delight because you don't have to be real careful as to how many tracks you're going to have to construct the composition."

With all these toys at his disposal, O'Hearn still considers it important to season electronic textures with a dash or two of acoustic spice. "In late '81, I did *Ancient Dreams* as an all-electronic album because there wasn't so much of that going on back then. I even hung my bass guitars on the wall. But now there's so much electronic stuff going on, I tried to introduce some other instruments on *Rivers Gonna Rise.*"

When asked about new age music, O'Hearn sighed as that label raised its mellow head again. "I'm not sure what new age means," he says. "If someone can use certain music to meditate or get a little jolt in their imagination, great. I'm all for it. But as a general blanket-type marketing term, it bugs me because I don't particularly care to be associated with so much of the stuff that falls under that umbrella. Sometimes it bothers me when someone makes that association, sometimes it doesn't. It depends on the day of the week, how late I stayed up the night before, how much coffee I've had to drink.

I'm just excited to see that instrumental music is getting such a break these days, regardless of all the dreck that's being released," he states. "I don't want to sound like a sourpuss. I'm not putting down anyone for doing what they want to do. But I am happy that this new age thing has given instrumental music a chance to stand up and be counted. It has allowed record companies to market instrumental music that doesn't technically fall into the jazz or rock bins in record stores."

Other developments in the music industry also give O'Hearn gounds for optimism. "What an age we're living in!" he smiles. "It's just amazing. I was listening to a tape of electronic stuff I was trying to do in 1979 or '80, and it really is good for a laugh. I was so sincere about it, but none of it is run by any central clock. It's just random, wild step-sequencing—eight- and 16-voice things that maybe overlap in some elliptical way every now and then and sync up for a few seconds. It was so frustrating, because you'd hear things like Kraftwerk's *Man Machine*, the consummate techno album of the '70s, and everything is just so perfect and in the pocket. To be inspired by that, then try to duplicate it and have it sound so God-awful, was really maddening.

"Finally I got my hands on an old Roland MC-4, and I was off and running. I overcame a tremendous tech-

no-hurdle and got into sequencing. That was big stuff in 1980 and '81. Around that same time, the EMT 250 digital reverb was the hot item in signal processing. Studios were paying about $20,000 for that thing. But it doesn't do a fraction of what a Yamaha REV7, or even a Lexicon PCM-70, will do. And with polyphonic MIDI sequencers available for $200 or $300, we've taken a quantum leap beyond the MC-4 too.

"So what a heyday for the home studios! Just pick up the classifieds, buy a used PCM-70 or REV7, and you're in business. Nowadays you can do a world-class recording in your garage, and put it up against studio stuff. It's so nice to be able to work whenever you want, rather than have someone tell you, 'Sorry, but Ozzy's in here this afternoon,' or work with an assistant engineer's second with a Megadeath T-shirt who listens to a few bars of your music and says, 'Whoa, dude, that was some pretty spacey shit!'"

And there's life beyond home studios too. At this very moment, O'Hearn is on the road with a trio. His mission: "To dispel the myth that the composer of this music is a faceless guy just sitting in his room. Most so-called new age guys don't play live, and most of those who do give concerts that are tantamount to gulping half a dozen Valium, as far as the audience is concerned. I want to do a real four-alarm show. It's all live. It would be nice to make use of the sequencer because some of these arrangements, especially the ones from the new album, are a little ambitious. But it's also nice to have the freedom to improvise, to let the tracks breathe dynamically without being locked into a click. It's nice to be able to extend. If a tune is working out just right and the audience is grooving, why not go ahead and stretch out a little?"

Good plan. Our bet is that O'Hearn onstage will definitely be worth the ticket.

Today, O'Hearn is an established solo artist, freed by modern musical technology from the treadmill of journeyman accompaniment. With three solo albums to his credit—*Ancient Dreams, Between Two Worlds,* and the recently-released *Rivers Gonna Rise*—he's churning out even more music in his home studio outside of L.A.

O'Hearn's debut in the film business, *Destroyer,* marks Rob Kirk's debut as a director, and football star Lyle Alzedo's premiere acting gig. He plays a mass murderer hiding out in the bowels of an abandoned prison, into which Anthony Perkins—yes, *the* Anthony Perkins—marches with a gaggle of frolicking actresses and a loopy crew to shoot something called *Babes Behind Bars.* "*Destroyer* is a hack-and-slash movie," he admits. "One of those projects that will probably wind up a skeleton in my closet someday."

Too bad *Phantom Of The Opera* beat *Destroyer* onto Broadway. But that shouldn't keep us from enjoying O'Hearn's handiwork. "Malone's Jump" underscores a scene in which a stunt actress climbs to a third-floor balcony inside the prison and, with Perkins' gnomes filming away, leaps out toward a mattress that may or may not be waiting below. "It's a happy little toe-tapper," O'Hearn says. "It seemed to work for the scene. The way the scene was cut seemed to demand something with a regular rhythm foundation, so I created a bass drum pulse on my Roland TR-505 at about 118 beats a minute, which worked quite well overall with the length of the cue.

"Then I started the ostinato figure on my PPG 2.2," he continues. "It's built on groups of seven notes, laid over the four-on-the-floor pulse. After that I introduced the melody on my Akai S900 and the bass line on the PPG—I think it's one of the bigger, heavier PPG programs, like Dragon Breath, with a lot of noise and hiss, doubled by a vocal sample on the S900."

There's a hi-hat pattern in "Malone's Jump" too, which O'Hearn believes he created on his old Oberheim SEM modules. "Those are the greatest things Oberheim ever built," he enthuses. "They do such wonderful electronic percussion sounds. I'm convinced that Kraftwerk got some of their classic sounds from SEMs and ARP 2600s. You can get everything from huge explosions to little hi-hats on the SEMs. My friend Wayne Yentis put a patch point into their filters, so I can get a truly dynamic hi-hat. As the filter opens and closes, it sounds like a hi-hat opening and closing, but very electronic. That's what's so cool about these instruments. With samplers, you're pretty much locked into what you sample; there's only so much manipulation you can do. I like having the ability to completely change my stuff live."

The SEM modules are also O'Hearn's first choice for bass lines. "I was using the Minimoog for quite a spell,

but it wasn't mine, although I do intend to get one," he says. "Now I use a combination of the SEMs for bass. They have their own character altogether. It's Moogish, but a little brighter and clearer than that wooly low Moog sound. That, in combination with the [Oberheim] Xpander and the 2600, does it for me. But since I came to the [Roland] D-50 a few months back, I've found that you can get a pretty nice bass sound on it too, especially in combination with the other analog stuff. The PPG also gets a hell of a bass sound, but it's more alien, with a real metallic quality."

O'Hearn is comfortable with his gear, which mixes old and new on the basis of what sounds best to him, rather than what is this week's Axe Of The Decade. He approaches each item in his studio with full awareness of its strengths and limitations, and develops clear notions about how it can best be used. "The PPG covers a lot of melody parts," he says. "It does simple triad voicings too, because it's only a four-voice instrument in stereo, which is how I like to run it.

"The Roland D-50 and MKS-70 are used primarily for pads; they don't play too many melodies, except maybe in tandem with the PPG and the other Roland instruments. The MKS-70 is great for string-like, square-wave stuff, just like the Xpander. I was sorry to see that it doesn't have any kind of pulse width device, though. You've got fixed sawtooth, triangle, and square waves, and that's it, good luck. An analog synthesizer without pulse width variation is a sorry beast. I mean, the pulse width variance on the old Oberheim SEM stuff and the 2600 is superb. You can get the square wave down to sound like a BB on a bongo, as well as a full, rich square wave sound." □

A Selected Patrick O'Hearn Discography
Solo albums (on Private Music): *Ancient Dreams*, 2002; *Between Two Worlds*, 2017; *River's Gonna Rise*, 2029. **With others:** *World Of Private Music Sampler*, 2009-1-P9.

DAVID QUALEY

By Mark Hanson

Imagine following fingerstyle guitar legend Leo Kottke onto the stage after a standing ovation and two encores. Not an enviable position for any guitarist. But Windham Hill recording artist David Qualey did just that at the August 1987, American Finger-Style Guitar Festival in Milwaukee, Wisconsin—and acquitted himself very nicely, to boot.

The 39-year-old Qualey earned an ovation and an encore of his own with a performance of original nylon-string guitar instrumentals, ranging from the blazing "Ride Of The Headless Horseman" to the exquisitely understated "Winter's Palace," a musical depiction of falling snowflakes. Qualey's whimsical sense of humor, flawless technique, and unique compositions made for an impressive evening of listening.

An American living in Germany, Qualey has recorded five albums for the European labels Stockfisch and Teldec. Windham Hill Records founder Will Ackerman heard him while on tour in Europe during 1978, and was impressed enough to ask him for the licensing rights to Qualey's second German release, *Guitar Solo.* The licensing agreement never materialized, but Qualey, who had retained the rights to his music, simply re-recorded the album for Windham Hill. It was released in 1980 as *Soliloquy.* Qualey's recording of "Jesu, Joy Of Man's Desiring" is included on Windham Hill's 1986 sampler LP, the Grammy-nominated *Winter's Solstice.*

With a solid reputation in Europe, Qualey currently plays 300- to 500-seat halls across the continent, most often performing *without* amplification. "When I travel, I don't carry any musical equipment with me besides my guitar," Qualey says. "I don't worry about amplifying the guitar because I almost never have to use amplification. The first club gig I did in Germany was a breakthrough of sorts. I had to convince the club owner to let me try playing in his place. He thought it would never work, because his patrons were always so noisy. But when I sat down to play, all the noise stopped. They really paid attention to the music. And it's been like that ever since."

Qualey is something of an enigma among nylon-string guitarists. Although he plays with the technique of a trained classical guitarist, he never studied classical guitar. (However, he does admit to having studied

Frets, March 1988

the Carcassi Etudes for classical guitar at one point.) His repertoire consists entirely of his own compositions—harmonically conservative, yet beautiful pieces that fit much more easily into the new age mold than into the standard classical repertoire. He also taps his foot when he plays. See if you can find professional classical players anywhere with tapping toes.

Unable to make a satisfactory living in the United States as a performer, the Oregon-born Qualey went to Europe with the hope of supporting himself doing nothing but performing and recording his guitar instrumentals. "I was very frustrated having to sing the most recent John Denver tune to get work," Qualey remembers, "so I left for England and Germany in 1974. A friend who was in the service had advised me to come over. So my family and I packed up and went. It was more like chasing the pot of gold at the end of the rainbow than following solid business leads, but it certainly has worked out over the years."

Qualey's early influences included Chet Atkins. "I was about 11 when I started playing in earnest," he says. "I had taken a few lessons on a Silvertone with impossible action, but I quit after a few months. I heard Chet's 'Baubles, Bangles, and Beads' [*Travelin'*, RCA LPM-2678, out of print] the next year and got hooked. I had no sense of rhythm, and I couldn't play the chops at all, but I loved it. I began practicing at home by myself, and developed a very personal relationship with the guitar.

"Two years later I *saw* Chet playing 'Windy And Warm' [*This Is Chet Atkins*, RCA, VPS-6030] on TV," Qualey recalls, "and finally realized how he was playing all of those notes at once. The alternating bass had eluded me up to that point, but once I saw him do it, it all started making more sense."

Qualey's budding guitar career developed in jazz- and rock-band settings through high school, highlighted by a first prize at a California state battle of the bands at the age of 16. "I was playing a Gibson 330 [a double cutaway semi-hollow electric guitar similar to its more famous cousin, the ES-335] at that time," Qualey says. "Shortly after that I was under contract to RCA with a rock band. We had some potential, but I had gotten hooked on the classical guitar after hearing a two-guitar arrangement of [Debussy's] 'Claire de Lune.' I quit the band I was in and started working on the classical music."

The Vietnam-era military draft also promised to hook Qualey. He chose to enlist for a three-year stint, landing a desk job that allowed him time to practice

and to perform. "That led me into lounge work where I had to sing as well as play," Qualey says. "I didn't want to sing, and one time I actually ended up telling off an audience for not listening. I didn't do much work for that agency after that, but I got a great gig as the house guitarist at The Guitar, a 40-seat listening bar in Manhattan [Jazz great] Jim Hall, among others, played there. Unfortunately, it closed in 1973, which was about when I took off for Europe."

A work permit problem in England nearly sidetracked Qualey's European career before it got started. "I couldn't stay in England because of the foreign-worker situation," Qualey remembers, "so I wound up in Germany not knowing a word of the language. I started playing on the streets. I was able to record some of my arrangements of pop tunes for a radio station in northern Germany. I took the payment and ran, figuring that I would never hear about it again. But they started playing the pieces on the air, which gained me some notoriety. It also led to a recording contract with the Stockfisch label."

All of Qualey's recording is done in his home studio in the countryside of northern Germany. "My studio is a one-man operation," Qualey says. "I was able to buy the equipment with the advance for the second record. I have an Atari 1/2" 8-track recorder. My studio is digital quality now. I'm spending some time with MIDI, for ease in writing and composing."

The recording process is not a painstaking, note-by-note process for Qualey. "I won't try to record a tune more than once a day," he says. "If I don't get it quickly, then I'll move on to something else. The spirit has to be in the music when I record it. If I play it too many times in a row it loses its feeling. I seldom overdub. I'm a fanatic for clean playing, but I'll never splice two different takes together."

Qualey has a similar outlook concerning his daily regimen. "I won't practice a piece more than once a day, either" he says. I generally warm up by playing through about half of my performance repertoire. The other half I'll do the next day. Then I'll work on new material, and do whatever recording I have planned for the day. I never warm up before a concert with the pieces that I'm going to perform. I want the feeling to be fresh when I'm onstage.

"I compose with the guitar in my lap," Qualey continues. "My compositional approach is very improvisational. My pieces are built on the guitar, although I'm improving at working out musical ideas in my head."

Most of Qualey's compositoins are full-bodied in texture. "I'm very much a chordal worker," he says. "I like full-sounding guitar music. It's a very pianistic approach in a way. I view each of my compositions as a balloon: I can't pull out part of it without the whole thing collapsing. I avoid single lines. I like to have harmony at all times. I think I would be totally lost in unharmonized modes."

Which guitarist is Qualey listening to currently? "I live in a vacuum in the guitar world," he says. "I grew up listening to my own guitar, not so much to the stars of the day. It's still that way for me. I live with my instrument, not with other players." □

A Selected David Qualey Discography
Solo albums (on Windham Hill): *Soliloquy*, WH-1011; *Sampler '81*, WH-1015; *Winter's Solstice*, WHj-1045. (On Stockfisch [Sandornweg 3-b, 3300 Braunschweig, West Germany]): *Guitar Parables*, 5025. (On Teldec [Heussweg 25, 2000 Hamburg 13, West Germany]): *Guitar Solo*, 6.23413 AS; *Awhile Ago*, 6.25142 AO; *Reflections*, 6.25949 AS.

"One-Time Swing (Two-Time Fling)"

By David Qualey

David Qualey's "One-Time Swing (Two-Time Fling)" uses arpeggio patterns (measures 1-6 and 15-22, for example) and an alternative bass (measures 7-11 and 28-38). At times he uses both picking styles in a single measure (measures 12 and 14). The tune, which can be found on his *Reflections* album, is played with a swing feeling.

In measure 6, finger the third, fourth, and fifth strings with the index; bend it backward slightly to allow the open second string to ring. In measures 29-38, you'll find right-hand harmonics; the standard notation shows pitches an octave *lower* than normal for the harmonics, for ease in reading. If right-hand harmonics are difficult for you, they may be played as regular fretted notes at the written pitches.

In measures 39-48 many of the alternate bass notes (second and fourth beats) are played as a chordal strum with the thumb, in the style of Merle Travis and Chet Atkins. These chords could be pinched with the thumb and fingers instead.

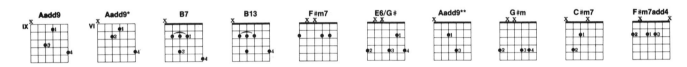

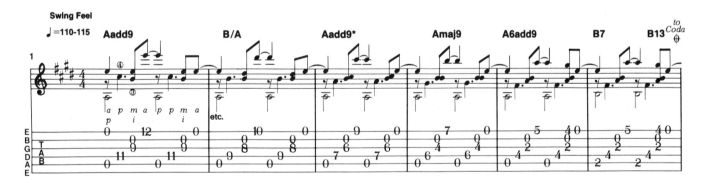

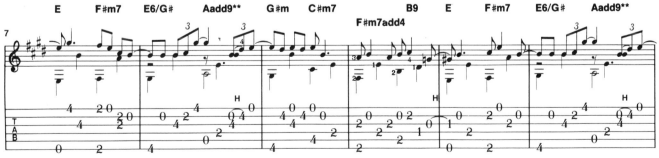

Music Continued

Continued From Previous Page

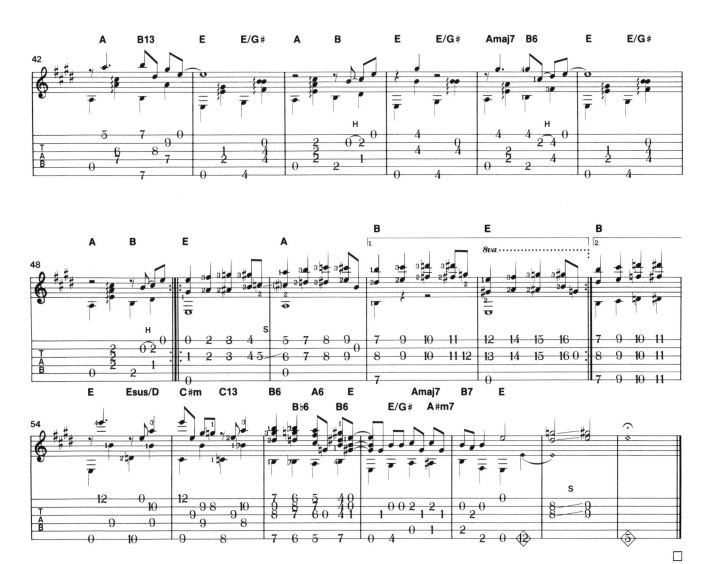

PHILIPPE SAISSE

By Bob Doerschuk

Keyboard, October 1988

Mick Jagger, Chaka Khan, and Nile Rodgers are seldom mistaken for new age musicians. So how did Philippe Saisse manage to segue from a busy session routine with these and a score of other rock/rhythm-and-blues heavyweights to the airy heights of new age notoriety?

Saisse laughs. "Beats me. Chaka is definitely not a soft singer. Neither are the Stones. Niles does high-energy stuff. And I live in New York, a very high-energy city. That's probably why I did *Valerian* [Windham Hill (Dist. by A&M), 1073]—it was a nice relief."

And, to those who have been following Saisse's career, a surprise as well. Eleven years ago, after graduating from the Paris National Conservatory, performing with the Paris Symphony Orchestra, moving to the U.S. to study with vibraphonist Gary Burton at Berklee, and apprenticing with producer Narada Michael Walden, the French-born keyboardist/percussionist began burning a path to the top of the rock session heap. In addition to Khan, Jagger, and Rodgers, Saisse has sizzled on disc with David Bowie, Billy Joel, Steve Winwood, Grace Jones, Brian Wilson, and Hall & Oates, among others. His reputation for mixing chops, taste, and relentless drive has spread throughout the industry.

But in the midst of his hectic routine, while catching his breath between studio dates, a strange thing happened to Saisse. "I was at this country-style restaurant in my neighborhood," he remembers, "and suddenly I noticed this peaceful music on the house system. When I asked the waiter what it was, he gave me this weird look and said, 'Don't you know? This is a Windham Hill sampler.' I said, 'Oh. Okay.' Then, a few weeks later, the same thing happened somewhere else. By this time, I was really wondering what in the world a Windham Hill sampler was. As far as I was concerned, it seemed like a pretty weird name for a band."

Over the next few months, Saisse learned about the label and the musical philosophy with which it is often associated. He saw an Andreas Vollenweider concert at Radio City Music Hall, and left impressed with the good vibes the harpist shared with his audience. Certainly some flavor of this music lingered in his memory as Saisse began work on *Valerian,* although he insists that he never consciously molded the music along new age stylistic lines, or even considered making it his debut solo album.

"I didn't do *Valerian* because of a need to express myself," he says. "I was in two bands—one was Doppelganger, and the other was Out Loud, with Nile Rodgers—and I was expressing myself a lot with them. The only purpose behind *Valerian* was to see what would happen if I let myself loose in my studio for fun. What would I spontaneously come up with?"

What he came up with was a hit. Released on Windham Hill, *Valerian* was Saisse's ticket onto the adult contemporary charts. Its soft textures, flowing themes, gently percolating rhythms, and overall polish, combined with the tranquility of the music in his favorite restaurants, add up to an ideal formula for airplay in the late '80s. The album's success pleases Saisse, though he is quick to point out that his motivation for doing it was anything but commercial.

"The most important thing I kept in focus while doing *Valerian* was that I was doing it to please myself, without fitting it into a category. When I'm producing Sanborn or Al Jarreau or whoever, I always put myself into categories. When I did *Destiny* [Warner Bros., 25425] with Chaka, the focus was on getting another 'I Feel For You.' *Valerian* was the first project I've ever done that didn't have A&R people from some label breathing down my neck and saying, 'We need a single!'"

The album's popularity also had an unexpected side effect. Saisse has abandoned his studio tan for occasional excursions onto the concert stage, including several recent gigs in Japan. There, he was interrogated by dozens of journalists, all preoccupied with the question of what new age is all about. While Saisse considers himself a rocker with only tenuous connections to the mellow side of music, he acknowledges that he has been influenced by new age, and that this influence has been beneficial.

"To be realistic, a lot of new age musicians don't

have a lot of technique or knowledge," he says. "People like George Winston are very talented; they have their thing down. But there are others who follow that lead and try to cash in on it. It's like, 'I'll buy this D-50; that'll sound nice on my new age record.' But they don't have the chops to do anything with it.

"Why not have somebody with total chops, total musicianship, do this kind of stuff? We don't have to use complicated time signatures and harmonies. You don't have to play a million notes a minute, like the Berklee speed-freak school from the old jazz fusion days. Why is it that so many proficient musicians do unnerving music? A lot of the music I enjoy is very unnerving to my girlfriend, for example. But whenever I put on something by Vollenweider, it's pleasant for both of us. The new age thing made me realize that you can do music that lets you use everything you have to create something interesting *and* pleasant."

True to this spirit, Saisse emphasized freedom and looseness on *Valerian*, as opposed to the perfection he pursues on commercial projects. This even affected his approach to synthesizer orchestration. "Normally on a session, I try to stay away from stock sounds," he explains. "I would never use one synth to get one sound; I try to be more creative than that. But *Valerian*

isn't about trying to be ten times better for myself than I am for Chaka or Sanborn. I wasn't concerned with getting the most beautiful harp sound in the world by MIDIing three or four different things. It was more important to play live, so I needed to have every synth play one part. If the basic D-50 harp sound was good, with maybe a little tweaking, fine. What the harp was playing, and how I played it, was more important. Same thing with the piano sound. Although as a producer on other people's records I'd normally go wild over that, I didn't worry at all about miking the piano on *Valerian*. Yet it sounds really good—because I only came in to play, without worrying about anything else. I was content just listening to one note being played."

No worries. Letting the music run free. Going with the flow. Taking life one note at a time. Is Saisse on his way to joining the new age parade after all?

Not quite. "*Valerian* hasn't taken over my normal activities, which are still very much pop and R&B. My everyday life is still more into commercial music. I'm still kind of the outcast of the Windham Hill label. I haven't even met Will [Ackerman, president of Windham Hill]! Sure, Will's records, and stuff by Philip Aaberg, are kind of relaxing, because there's nothing much there to analyze.　□

RICHARD SOUTHER

By Bob Doerschuk

Keyboard, May 1986

Not too long ago, Richard Souther was banged up in an automobile accident. A couple of years before that, he survived a bout with botulism. Most impressive of all, he continues to bear up to the rigors of a career as a studio musician. He's a resilient sort, though. Physically, he's doing just fine now. And spiritually, he's on top of the world, judging by the beatific vibes of his debut solo album, *Heirborne* [Meadowlark (dist. by Sparrow Corp., Chatsworth, CA 91311), 7004].

Souther, a veteran keyboardist whose credits include sessions with Al Jarreau, Joni Mitchell, Debby Boone, and Barry McGuire, straddles several styles on this all-synthesizer LP, but the new age label seems to fit most comfortably. "My producer, Peter York, had a lot to do with that," the 34-year-old artist explains. "I submitted about 41 pieces of music for him to choose from for this album. A lot of it had more funk and '2-4' to it, but Peter felt that the mood he and the president of the company wanted to convey was summed up in

the songs we both wound up picking."

Meadowlark is an outgrowth of Sparrow, an established Christian label. According to Souther, Meadowlark hopes to build a reputation as a monument to instrumental music written and recorded by spiritually-oriented musicians. "I've worked with Sparrow for years," he says. "I think they wanted to create an opportunity to showcase people like myself, who write but don't sing. The idea, though, is to go for a unique sound, just as Windham Hill did, so that you think of the label and the quality it represents more than of the artist on the label."

On their early albums, Windham Hill emphasized simple musical settings: solo piano or acoustic guitar, for instance. In contrast, the tranquil ambience on *Heirborne* was created with a roomful of electronic gear, all of which is listed on the jacket cover. Some of it isn't actually on the album, such as the Yamaha CS-80, left out at the last minute because it hadn't been MIDIed, and the two Oberheim Xpander modules; the jacket art had already been finished when Souther remembered he hadn't used the Oberheims after all. And there is no sampling, simply because he got his first sampling machine, an E-mu Emulator II, too late. That still leaves a formidable lineup of instruments that Souther mobilized for his meditative mission.

There are several surprises behind the making of *Heirborne*. One involves the studio. The recording quality of *Heirborne* is top-notch, yet all of it was done in Souther's living room. Even more impressive, the entire session took only two days to do. To Richard, however, doing a two-day album project amidst couches and coffee tables makes perfect sense.

"I have an immense amount of equipment," he explains. "On another project, I tried hauling everything out of my place to a studio, and it was a nightmare. It took literally a day to set everything up, and then we had to troubleshoot: 'Why isn't this cable connected properly,' and all that. So using my place seemed the most logical thing to do."

The fact that there wasn't any recording gear in his living room didn't slow Souther down. Arrangements were made for Tim Pinch to park his mobile 24-track studio outside. "Tim and Peter York were in Tim's remote truck, and Eric Persing, who programmed my instruments for me, and I were inside. We could communicate with the truck via a video camera, with a pair of Ureis as monitors. It was pretty painless, because the bulk of the music was completed. It had all been sequenced. I'd even taken it through a few trial runs

the week before to conserve even more session time."

One reason why the session went so quickly was that, aside from his prerecorded sequences, Souther played practically everything else live. "We used all 16 MIDI channels," he says. "There were only two overdubs. I added one flute line, and later, during mixdown at [guitarist/producer] Larry Carlton's studio, I overdubbed a bell part I had totally forgotten about at the session. We used a Roland SBX-80 sync box with SMPTE and click, so we could offset when we laid down the tracks. We would go back, sometimes do two or three passes, and pretty much lock everything up. You can hear some MIDI delays, especially on the [Roland] MSQ 700 in chain mode, when it goes from section to section, but that's cool."

The sequences in *Heirborne* are gentle, never disrupting the music's soft contours. "I'd say about 70 percent of the sequences were done in step time," Souther estimates. "I learned a lot about step time when I was recovering from botulism. My adrenalin system had shut off, and I had lost most of the ability to do mechanical things. Now, of course, I don't use step time if I need to get a part letter-perfect. I'll just slow down the MSQ and play the part real slow instead.

"The MSQ was my workhorse on the album," he continues. "The only limitation you have is its capacity of 6,500 bits of information. So I bounced from that to a Roland MSQ 100. It was kind of like using an 8-track and a 2-track. The system was very dependable."

A number of different drum machines turned up on *Heirborne* too. "It wasn't planned," Souther insists. "It just happened that way. About two months prior to doing the record, I had gotten hold of a Linn 9000, so I transferred most of the stuff that had already been written on the LinnDrum for percussion and effects, but my main drum machine was the 9000. The Sequential Tom is on there too. It's just a stereo out, but you can control it in all sorts of neat ways from a keyboard, panning it, doing different tunings, and programming it all into your sequencer."

Even with all the drum machines, Souther brought in Alex Acuna to play some additional percussion parts. "He came to Larry Carlton's on the day we mixed," Richard says, "and added some percussion, some hi-hat, and some cymbals. That helped get rid of the mechanical side of the drum machines and add a little human sparkle. We had thought about bringing in a bass player, too, but in retrospect we found that there wasn't a need for one. The sounds we got by combining the 360 Systems MIDI Bass with a Minimoog and

[Yamaha] DX7 worked real well. I especially love the bass on the title track; Eric calls it his Jaco patch."

Perhaps the dominant sound in *Heirborne*'s collage of textures is the Casio CZ-101 flute sound, heard first on the opening cut, then recurring on other melody lines elsewhere. "Eric Persing came up with that," Souther says. "He calls it his Fairlight flute sound. It just happened that a lot of the music that was picked for *Heirborne* had that sound on it, which delighted me. I love that particular sound; it's inspired a lot of my ideas. Sometimes I used it on two CZ-101s, MIDIed and detuned. Elsewhere on the record, I ran the two CZs with different sounds."

Since MIDI played such a major part in the *Heirborne* session, Souther was particular about choosing a keyboard controller. He wound up using a Roland MKB-1000, partly because of its ability to send out on two MIDI channels at once for layering effects. But the feel of the keys was important too, and the weighted action helped sell Richard on the MKB as well.

Though the execution and conception of *Heirborne* reflect Souther's comfort with electronics, the piano was his major instrument practically from infancy. A bona fide prodigy, he began taking lessons at age three and gave his debut recital at four. But a teacher with a strict disciplinarian approach soured a 12-year-old Richard on the piano and helped steer him toward alternative keyboards.

"I lost all desire to study classical music after that," he remembers. "The intense pressure of trying to do it perfect every time was just too much. And that's fine. I've gone down a path I probably wouldn't have explored otherwise. I still record solo piano music [*Ed. Note: Souther has a solo piano LP out under the pseudonym Douglas Trowbridge, titled* Songs Unspoken (*Meadowlark, 7007*)], and the classical side comes through there. But because I wrote *Heirborne* on synthesizers, I found that the writing technique I came up with was totally different. The textures I could get by combining different synthesizers became my springboard. When I write on piano, the melody is what usually comes to me first. But the textures I get when writing on synthesizers trigger a different kind of creative process."

Using technology to stimulate untapped creative resources, creating soothing music for modern times on modern instruments—perhaps Souther has stumbled across the most relevant formula yet for music from the *truly* "new age." ☐

LIZ STORY

By Bob Doerschuk

Keyboard, July 1984

Windham Hill broke into the record world in 1976 as the personal flagship of founder/guitarist Will Ackerman. His mellow style, and the stable of finger-pickers he recruited for his company's first projects, encouraged an early perception of the label as a haven for a new generation of 6-string folkies.

That preconception changed with the success of George Winston, whose rise to prominence confirms that Windham Hill has plenty of room for pianists as well. A number of them have recorded on the label: Bill Quist's *Piano Solos Of Eric Satie* [Windham Hill (dist. by A&M), 1008] remains the label's only release containing no original compositions written by the performer, while Barbara Higbie's duet LP with violinist Darol Anger [*Tideline*, 1021], Scott Cossu's ensemble effort *Wind Dance* [1061], Ira Stein's soaring improvisations with oboist Russel Walder [*Elements*, 1020], and Winston's triptych [*Autumn*, 1012;

Winter Into Spring, 1019; and *December,* 1025] are all tributes to Ackerman's faith in their ability to blossom in the open fields of free creativity through the sounds and textures of the piano.

But Liz Story is the only Windham Hill pianist [*Ed. Note: Liz Story is currently with RCA's new age label, Novus*], other than Winston to come out with a solo disc featuring primarily original material. *Solid Colors* [1023] exhibits her mastery of the label's familiar style, which is consonant in melody, flowing in rhythm, and evocative in texture. Yet she is no Winston Clone. Where George has a percussive attack, her touch is legato, and her soaring runs contrast with his gently angular designs.

She got involved with Windham Hill through a three-tune demo tape she had sent to the company as a result of a friend's urgings. It was the first demo tape she had ever mailed, yet it was enough to prod Ackerman into giving her a call. "At the time I had no experience with record companies, so it has only been since talking with other people and becoming more aware of the music business that I've been amazed at how fortunate I was to hook up with people who are this enlightened," she states.

Story developed her fresh extemporaneous style mainly through her long tenancy at a Los Angeles restaurant, where she played a weathered upright whose music rack had been removed long before. "There was no place to put the music," she recalls, "so I couldn't do requests. I didn't even play classical music, since I hadn't memorized the pieces I could do. So I just sat and played."

The experience polished her improvisational skills. She had improvised at home, but the pressure of playing before an audience added a different dimension to her explorations. "At home I was just fooling around," she says, "but in the restaurant I committed myself to establishing a beginning, a middle, and an end. Instead of getting up for a cup of coffee, I had to sit there for three or four hours and get involved in the themes and ideas that would come up. A couple of songs, like 'Bradley's Dream,' just came out one night. The whole album actually evolved during that year and a half of playing in the restaurant."

Eventually the restaurant gig lost its allure; Liz decided to leave after receiving a request to play "Autumn In New York," a song she didn't know, playing another piece instead, and then receiving the oblivious listener's thanks for her rendition of "Autumn In New York." "It was like a real revelation that the atmosphere there just wasn't right anymore," she recalls, "that the connection I needed as a performer wasn't there." She took with her a library of material evolved there for use in *Solid Colors* and future projects. Story locked most of it in her memory, notating only the most inspired ideas. Now that she's started work on her second album, though, she is writing a bit more down.

Her new interest in developing themes, rather than simply stringing them together in a musical stream of consciousness, stems also from her ongoing study with the classical pianist and composer Bernardo Seagall. In these lessons, Story seeks to combine her love of improvising with the discipline of her early training. Her first teachers discouraged her from making up her own material, and drilled her on written repertoire instead. This constrictive approach led to occasional problems and teeth-gnashing episodes, perhaps the most harrowing being her performance of a 30-minute concerto that she had memorized in sequence; one mistake, and she would have been forced to go back to the beginning.

It took what Liz calls a "somewhat religious experience" to shake her loose from this rote routine and lift her into the airy realm of extemporaneous performance. That experience was a chance encounter with the late jazz pianist Bill Evans at the Bottom Line in New York. "The idea of improvisation hadn't even occurred to me," she says, "until that night. I had never heard jazz, so it wasn't even on a level of saying, 'Oh, those are interesting voicings.' I didn't have any idea what he was doing, but I could see that he clearly understood the piano as a kind of vocabulary I had never heard, and that he was saying what he wanted to say."

On Evans' recommendation, Liz launched into eight months of study with Sanford Gold, focusing on harmony, running through diminished scales, arranging standards, and getting progressively depressed at her inability to put these puzzle pieces together into an expressive whole. After moving to Los Angeles and studying there with Jack Scalese and at the Dick Grove Music Workshops, she began to find that the key for her was to allow free rein to her improvisatory impulses. "It's like being inspired by a French poetry reading if you don't understand French," she says. "You might decide that you want to write French poetry, so you try to learn the language, which is a whole different process from actually doing the writing. I was learning this language, all this harmony and theory; it took another period of time to set all that aside and let ideas flow out of me. It took me a while to learn to be comfortable with a piece like 'White Heart,' which just came out of me all of a sudden one day. It was so simple and sweet that I was almost embarrassed by it. I really wanted to play like Joanne Brackeen."

Her work with Seagall takes this a step further. Rather than analyze structure in the pieces they study, they concentrate on the feeling behind the notes and the listening process that uncovers them. This concern for the organic in music affects her studio and stage attitude as well. Liz never listens through headphones while recording, preferring to leave mixing board wizardry to the producer. When performing live, she leaves sound checks up to the engineers, and insists on playing without monitors. She does like to have at least half an hour before each concert to familiarize herself with the instrument. These days she finds that her preference for large pianos is usually respected. Though the ideal piano remains an elusive sylph—it would have to have, she affirms, a Steinway bass, a Baldwin treble, and a Yamaha action—Liz comes across such sumptuous delights as her current favorite, a nine-foot Steinway in Portland, Maine, more often than before. And the unwelcome shocks—like the Yamaha CP-70 in a Chicago club that impelled her to retitle her pieces "New Electric This" and "New Electric That"—are less frequent bumps in her artistic road.

In addition to new recordings, Liz continues her live appearances and her free-flowing writing and improvising. That aspect of her music seems unlikely to change. "I like to remember something that Schoenberg said once," she laughs. "When asked about the directions in which he expected to move following the impact he had made on composition, he said, 'You know, there is still a lot of great music that needs to be written in *C* major.'" □

A Selected Liz Story Discography
Solo albums: *Part Of Fortune*, Novus (dist. by RCA), 3001-1-N9. (On Windham Hill): *Solid Colors*, 1023; *Unaccountable Effect*, 1034. **With others** (on Windham Hill): *An Evening With Windham Hill Live*, 1026; *Windham Hill Sampler '86*, 1048.

TANGERINE DREAM

By Ted Greenwald

Keyboard, November 1988

I f you create something ten years ago, and all of a sudden it becomes famous, it's quite funny, really," Edgar Froese states in his thick German accent. But Froese is not laughing. Rather, the visionary leader of Tangerine Dream is describing his frustration that the music he pioneered in the early days of synthesizers has become identified with the style known as new age. Paul Haslinger, a member of the group since 1985, concurs: "If any of Tangerine Dream's music could be called 'new age,' it would be the albums between 1974 and 1977."

In the 20 years that Froese has been using the name, Tangerine Dream has maintained a distinctive identity that, aside from its roots in late-'60s psychedelic rock, owes little to any other music in the world. Froese bristles when people miss that crucial point. "I understand it," he sighs, "but I don't like it."

"We don't like to be styled," Haslinger adds. "We like to freak out."

Though you might not know it from the spacious but tightly controlled sonorities of their latest album, *Optical Race*, freaking out was once T-Dream's specialty. Their free-form psychedelic jams, coming at a time when electronic instruments had been the sole province of the avant-garde wing of academia, showed that such devices could be used in rock—and not as gimmicks, either, but as the foundation of the sound.

The band began as Froese's vehicle for realizing in sound the tenets of surrealism espoused by his friend and mentor, painter Salvador Dali. Aiming to lay bare the bedrock of the imagination, Tangerine Dream cut loose the anchors of rock and roll—electric guitars, drums, and song structures—and headed for the uncharted horizon of synthesizer technology. During the latter years of the '70s, when Jean-Michel Jarre, Vangelis, Synergy, Kraftwerk, and the other rock-based synthesists were developing their craft, they were building on a foundation established by Tangerine Dream.

The group's early music pushed the modular synthesizers and analog sequencers of the time to the limits of their live performance capabilities. In contrast to other synthesizer players of the era, Tangerine Dream understood the synthesizer not as a keyboard, but as a collection of devices for producing and controlling sounds. On such records as their classic commercial breakthrough *Phaedra*, envelope generators shaped not just individual note events, but entire phrases. Clock pulses drove sequenced rhythms and articulated improvised chords. Disregarding the structures of conventional musical thought and practice, the group created fluid landscapes in which pitches, timbres, and rhythms collided and melted into one another, washing over static harmonic centers that ebbed and flowed in tides of undifferentiated sound.

Froese does not regard himself as a keyboard player (although Haslinger is a conservatory-trained pianist). The leader sees his lack of training as a balancing factor that makes for stronger music. "We have to understand what is needed artistically and what is there [in the music] just to make me think, 'I'm a very good keyboardist.' Fortunately, we've totally erased the ego-tripping aspect out of the band. Everybody can show what he can really do, but that shouldn't be the main purpose."

In contrast to many electronic ensembles, Tangerine Dream has always been a performing band, and another aspect of their pioneer status consists in bringing technology primarily designed for the studio into concert halls, festival grounds, and cathedrals. Their mastery of electronic music performance is documented on six live records, the latest of which, *Live-miles*, captures recent performances in Albuquerque, New Mexico, and West Berlin. At the same time, their studio output has been prolific, spanning 17 albums, not to mention Froese's numerous solo efforts.

In recent years, Tangerine Dream has been most visible—or rather, audible—in movie theaters rather than concert halls. The group's 1977 score for William Friedkin's *Sorcerer* rocketed them into high demand as film composers, a field in which Froese's original visual conception of the music found a direct application. Eleven feature-length movies later (including the hit

Risky Business), Tangerine Dream is still a hot ticket in Hollywood, having caused considerable controversy when they were hired to replace veteran film composer Jerry Goldsmith's soundtrack for *Legend*. Their latest score, for *Miracle Mile*, hit the screens in August '88.

In March (1988), Christoph Franke, a member of Tangerine Dream for 17 years, left to pursue a career in hardware development. "He recently collaborated with WaveFrame in Denver, Colorado," Froese explains. "We felt obliged to remain in pure music." Franke's replacement is Ralf Wadephal, a Berliner whose playing caught Froese's ear. "The Berlin keyboard scene is quite active," Froese points out, "so finding him was easy. We are lucky that he worked on the same equipment that we do, and that he is on the same musical level that we are." Having been with the group for such a short time, Wadephal appears on only one track of *Optical Race*. The new album is something of a reunion, since it was released on the Private Music label; Private Music president Peter Baumann played in the group between 1971 and 1977.

Wadephal wasn't able to join our conversation, which took place as the group prepared for a month-long North American tour. Froese and Haslinger, though, were on hand and brimming with perspectives on the state of technology, the state of music, and the intersection between them. Having helped to bring synthesizers out of the technological basement onto the stage and into the musical consciousness of the world, Tangerine Dream is now poised on the brink of MIDI's next generation, champing at the bit to leap into the void.

* * * *

*W*hen Tangerine Dream began concertizing, the music was mostly improvised. That doesn't appear to be the case any more.

Froese: Yes, that's true, mostly because we're working with the new technology. We began to re-evaluate when to improvise, and if there is any need to improvise, when we found that you cannot just close your eyes, press a button, and pray for the right sound or sequence to come out. Working with the new tech-

(Left to right) Ralf Wadephul, Paul Haslinger, Edgar Froese.

(Left to right) Paul Haslinger, Edgar Froese, and Peter Bauman.

nology means that you have to make programs and precompose things. During our previous American tour [excerpts of which appear on side one of *Livemiles*] we worked with the Yamaha QX1 sequencer. On the other side, in West Berlin, we worked with Atari computers and the Steinberg Pro-24 sequencer program.

Haslinger: For a live performance, you have to put the music in some format, and the most secure format at the time of the American tour seemed to be the QX1. It's a hardware unit, so you don't have to worry much about it. The Berlin concert was the first time we went onstage with computers. It doesn't really make a difference whether you use IBM, Mac, or Atari. But you do have to make it secure. Now we actually do dare to go onstage with computers.

How did the differences between the QX1 and the

Steinberg program affect the music you were able to produce?

Froese: Having 24 tracks of MIDI control, as we had on the Berlin concert, is very different from having only eight tracks with the QX1. With 24 tracks, you can have maybe 22 sound layers. The clock situation was better, too. Using the Steinberg synchronizer, we could synchronize things much more easily than we could with the SRC [SMPTE Reading Clock from Friend-Chip], which we used with the QX1. All of this made it much easier to create an interactive sound system.

Haslinger: The main difference between these two venues was that on the first, the Albuquerque concert, we had a very simple MIDI patch. We had just the QX1 as a master device, and our master keyboards in addition. We had our sync boxes, but nothing very seriously patched. It was just one line going around. On the Berlin concert, we used JL Cooper's MSB Plus, which we really like. It's simple, it does a lot, and it's reliable. We can set up any complex MIDI patch we need.

On your current tour, each player has two Atari Mega STs. How are they being used?

Haslinger: Each of us has a computer for sequences and another for sound storage, and each computer has a 20-meg hard drive. Each of us supplies the basic tracks for certain parts of the show, and we all interact with these by playing other parts. Although we have sys-ex data on the sequencer tracks, we have still the option of changing sounds with the other computer. The sequencer will hold 999 measures, and within that there might be five or six pieces. So we don't have to reload that often.

How much of the show is sequenced, and how much is live?

Haslinger: About 70 percent is strictly composed, and the other 30 percent is improvised.

The photo on the album cover of Livemiles *shows lots of diskettes sitting on top of your keyboards. Many bands would have somebody offstage loading those diskettes.*

Froese: We run everything ourselves. We still remember one very early gig when we used early sync machineries. We had external sync control by somebody who did our patch and our sample changes, and it was just horrifying. We need to have the control. Even if we do not improvise like in the old days, we love to have changes, and we love to jump into whatever creative process without asking somebody else to give it so much attention.

On Livemiles, *there's clearly some live playing mixed*

in with the sequences, but it's difficult to tell where one ends and the other begins.

Froese: We've got a philosophy about that: Everything that you can control with two hands—or better said, six hands—will be controlled with six hands. Beyond that, we obviously have to use sequencers.

Which sorts of things are sequenced, and which end up being performed by the six hands?

Froese: As you know, you can do everything with a sequencer, but to have a live feel, to have the feel of skill playing music, if you are a musician, you have to prove yourself. You have to have the enjoyment of being on a stage and responding to the audience. Therefore, you won't put too much preset information into the computer. So there is a wide range of possibilities left for us to interact. Sometimes the bass line is programmed, sometimes some noise stuff is programmed—specifically sounds, because it's hard to load them into a sampling machine in such a way that you can be sure they will hit at the right point. That's the hardest thing of all: to get those sound changes without any accident. With the QX1 it was nearly okay—I would say that 90 percent of it worked out pretty well, in fact.

Haslinger: There are three sequencer softwares which we use a lot and which are best for our needs. First, the Steinberg software, which comes with a lot of editors and librarians—you can manage your system pretty well just with that. For the Mac, it's still Peformer [from Mark Of The Unicorn], and for the PC, it's the Voyetra [Sequencer Plus] software. That doesn't mean that other softwares are not interesting for us. It just means that we're not that familiar with them. It's a personal instrument thing. These softwares really give us the feeling of being at home. Especially Steinberg— they are one hour's flight from Berlin. The guy who programmed the Pro-24 is a personal friend of ours, and we meet nearly every month to discuss things. He will address our points in the program, and that's a much more direct kind of contact than we have with Mac and PC programmers.

Froese: Obviously, the best would be to connect all three: the best of the Atari, the best of the IBM, and the best of the Mac. But as you may know, there are a few problems between the three of them, so we have to figure out what is the best facility for the stage, and we chose to go just with the Steinberg.

Is there something special that each computer offers?

Haslinger: Every machine and every program has its own advantages. We keep them all in the studio. If you're writing a song, or sequencing, or making up sounds, you need different aspects. We like to have the choice, and through the MIDI language we have the choice to simply play it over [one computer recording another computer's playback]. With the MIDI file formats coming up, we will be able to exchange disks between Mac softwares, between Atari softwares, and between IBM softwares.

What instruments are you playing live?

Haslinger: For the master keyboard, everybody has his own preference. Edgar plays a Roland RD-1000, Ralf plays a Yamaha KX88, and I play an old Roland MKB-300. I've carried it with me around the world. It's quite a funky instrument already, not good at all, but I like it. For sound devices, we use the Emax with the hard disk. It's just so practical. We're also using a couple of Akai S900s. Edgar and Ralf use the Roland S-550. Then we have the usual stuff, the TX816, the D-550 and D-110, and the Oberheim Matrix.

Edgar, you started as a guitarist rather than as a keyboard player.

Froese: I started as a very freaky blues guitarist. Then I changed in a more progressive way. The influence of Jimi Hendrix, obviously, brought me into that line. Then I forgot about playing the guitar for three or four years because Hendrix was just too much; I couldn't stand it. Then I started playing again, and today I love to add that sound that people can associate with immediately. I love to control those feels just by plucking a string and doing those fingerworkings.

Although Tangerine Dream is primarily a keyboard band, you don't make what would be called high-technique keyboard music. The music isn't designed to take advantage of the layout of the keyboard per se. Do you consider yourself a keyboard player?

Froese: I do not consider myself as anything except a composer. I don't want to be too philosophical about it, but I see everything as a life movie, and I try to express that life movie. It's the day-to-day life, and all the good and bad experiences are running through my very subjective personal filter and being hit with reflective thoughts and all of that sort of thing. I'm a very normal person. The only exception is that I reflect everything through the filter of music.

Paul, are you trained as a pianist, primarily?

Haslinger: I studied at the Academy in Vienna and piano was my main instrument. In a sense, my first love is the piano. But since the time I joined Tangerine Dream, I feel more like a composer. I do find, though, that since I'm trained on the keyboard, it is the most expressive interface for me. For getting into rhythmic structures, I like to play drums because of the physical approach, which is, especially for someone coming out of Europe, difficult to get. Listening to Indian or African percussionists, something arises in me saying, "I want that," and the way to approach it is combined with playing it. But I find that it's not possible for me to perform it perfectly, so the next step is to set up percussion and drum sound combinations on the master keyboard, so that I have a drum set on the keys. Whenever I go into rhythm, I start playing on drums and then go to the keyboard, because that's really my instrument. In a way I'm playing keyboard, and in a way I'm playing drums. I don't know how to call it—am I a keyboardist, or a drummer? I don't know, but keys are the way I like to express myself. I made different drum setups on the keyboard, so I can play them exactly as I want. Every drum on *Optical Race* is played in that way.

Do you use classical piano fingering technique, or do you play the keys from the forearm or wrist while holding a finger stiff?

Haslinger: Both. Sometimes I have to get into playing from my body, or I don't get the groove. But I do things with my fingers that frustrate every drummer. I play rolls using classical repeated-note technique. Sometimes things happen accidentally, too. I might try out the drum kit by playing a Chopin *Prelude*. People hear it, and they say, "How did you play that fill?"

Onstage, does each of you have specific kinds of tasks relating to musical structure, or do you each contribute freely with bass lines, melodies, accompaniments, drums, and so forth?

Haslinger: Sound-wise, the initial ideas for a piece come from one member. Most of the time, the one who does the initials for a song also does the basic structure for the live set, too. It runs on his machinery, and the basics come from his side. And, of course, we like to use the best side of each musical personality. In adjusting compositions for playing them live, we look for the best combination of predefinition, which you are stuck with, and having as much influence as possible during the performance. In every case it's different. Sometimes, just by adding a rhythm, you can make the whole thing feel dynamic. By adding a different harmony, you can shift it into a whole other atmosphere. By giving another melody on top, you can, for 95 percent of the people listening, make it another piece.

Froese: Now that we have the computer onstage, we can talk about it the evening before a concert and change the sound configuration.

You can't afford to lose any data while you're on tour. How do you deal with backups?

Froese: Usually we have the original and a couple of backup sets of disks. We try to be as safe as we can, but when you load a floppy that you have loaded ten or 20 times before, and all of a sudden you get the bloody error message, what can you do? It happens. We're waiting for a new data transmission format, so that maybe within the next two or three years we can forget about MIDI.

Haslinger: It's said to be behind the doors, already set. It's said to be 16-bit parallel and so on. [*Ed. Note: This is an entertaining rumor, but we checked with a couple of informed sources and were unable to verify it.*] On the other hand, the industry interest in MIDI is so broad that I don't think a more powerful standard has any chance in the next year, except in the bigger systems, which just go their own way.

Will these technological changes affect the kinds of music you create?

Froese: I would say—and I'm very sure about it—that music will have a new direction within the next five to six years. There will be two big categories: The traditional will be music as we know it, and then there will be a section that will be new music. That will be all kinds of music which will not be created by hand in the old-fashioned way, even if you use a a piano or a guitar. It will be controlled by a [computerized] system between the sound and the process of playing. You will have a generating aspect between the process of composing and the acoustic signal getting out of the speaker. The two types of music will drift away from each other. Obviously, some people will say, "The old music was the good music. I don't understand the new music. I can't relate to it." I will be absolutely happy if the people who love the old music will be tolerant about the others, and the others will be tolerant about the people who just want to listen to the acoustic guitar and the acoustic piano, which is great.

Could you explain a bit more about the difference between the "old music" and the "new music"?

Froese: If it's music that's coming out of a speaker system, people will just say, "Okay that's music." But in fact, the way of composing music is different if you have a controlling system between what you play by pressing a key and what you hear coming out of the speaker. If you play an acoustic guitar, or even a fuzz-tone guitar through an amp, that's a very direct process. But if there is a device between your idea and the speaker, it can change your idea 100 percent.

What you've been doing for a number of years is akin to that. Your setup, at least in the past, involved notes being articulated by a clock pulse rather than by your fingers, so that you chose the pitches with your fingers, but a machine selected the time they were to be played.

Froese: That's one point, but talk to musicians who are using computers. If they are honest, they will tell you that the improvised part in creating new sounds or sequencer lines is very, very high. For example, you are looking for a good bass guitar sound, and you end up sometimes with a brilliant Indian flute. It's because the way you search for a good sound brings you to a completely different field. All of a sudden, instead of hearing the bass line, which you have to play because you set it up with the drum part, you're hearing the flute sound, and you say, "Hey, that might make a good melody line." The chance of being creative and going in an opposite direction is very high. If you are open enough and not so distracted by it, it's a nice idea.

When you're working in the studio, do you compose a piece first and then find the sounds for it, or do the sounds inspire the piece?

Haslinger: It works both ways. When the D-50 came out, everybody was rushing to get one and get it in the studio. You would plug it in and play, and in the same moment you would have an idea. But of course it cannot always be like this, because there isn't a D-50 every day.

Did you share Chris Franke's involvement with WaveFrame? It seems that everyone is still waiting to see what their instrument will turn out to be.

Froese: We went through the Fairlight philosophy, the Synclavier philosophy, and so on. Those instruments are very good, no question about it. But for the music we work on and the philosophy we have about creating sounds, continuing to stay with one instrument for the next six or seven years . . . it's much easier for us to change everything every couple of months.

Haslinger: You get dependent when you only use one system. For our needs the main aspect is not the technical framework, but the musical aspect—how usable it is. There are a few sounds on the Synclavier and the Fairlight that we are able to approximate in other systems. We take the main sounds and transfer them to the Emulator II or other samplers. Techno-freaks will say that it's not the same sound because of the resolution and so forth, for us, music-wise, it makes sense.

Froese: We hate being told we have to spend sev-eral hundred thousand dollars on a piece of equipment just because it has a 16-bit sound and 32-channel recording and so on. I know the companies that make the systems spend a lot of money on research and a lot of money building them, and we respect that. They do a great job, but I think the future of music will be so different that it doesn't make sense to stick with a single approach to technology. A company may build a great system with advanced features, but while you're learning to use that very expensive machinery, its value has gone down to 20 percent of its original value. We bought several PPG WaveTerms a couple of years back for about $150,000 altogether. Within a year and a half we sold them for $20,000, because they were unreliable and the company was going bankrupt. That's a great deal of risk. I don't advise anybody to go out and do the same thing.

Haslinger: We are certainly following the Wave-Frame project with great interest. The people working on it have a great reputation, and they're hard workers. What I've found out so far is that the instrument has the same approach as all the 16-bit units coming out now. Everybody tries to get into 44.1kHz and 16-bit. What they don't understand is that it's not enough having so much memory, having so many possibilities, and being able to put a D-50, a DX7, and two E-II sounds together in the sampler. That's not the point. The point is, once you have the sound, you have to do something with it. I've played with the WaveFrame a couple of times, and what I heard is nice, but as soon as I wanted to add a bit of velocity or pitch-bend information, or whatever, it's not possible, you know? [*Ed. Note: According to a spokesman for WaveFrame, their AudioFrame sampler has both pitch-bending and velocity control of amplitude, but currently no velocity control over filter cutoff.*] It's always the same thing. As soon as it gets down to making music, these genius technicians say, "That's your job."

Froese: To be fair to WaveFrame, their machinery is brilliant. But those kids who want to create music today, whether they want to make a score, or a jingle, or to play in the garage next door, they should not forget that a composer, a real composer who has the music going on in his head, would not need a million-dollar equipment setup. He can buy a little home computer and a voice unit, and he can be much more effective than somebody else who needs a studio full of equipment.

Haslinger: The people I admire the most are the ones who are sitting at home with just a Casio SK-11, let's say, doing music that sounds so great that I'm

Tangerine Dream onstage in February 1980 concert.

ashamed. I know people who own a Synclavier just for the reputation, because they wouldn't get any jobs if they didn't. These are the two extremes, and the Casio guys really frustrate me, because they are doing such good music.

Froese: Kids of 15, 16, or 17 want to start making music because they love music, but they are led to think, "I have to become a big star, I have to have an agent, I have to have $100,000 to buy equipment." I want to make the statement that you do not have to have all of that to become a very good musician and composer. If you really have something to say to the world, one day you will have the chance. Maybe it takes a week, maybe it takes five years, but it will happen.

Do you still use your old modular gear?

Froese: Rarely. There is something very special about the old Moog filters. Every musician who has worked with those synthesizers knows that. We get very nice sounds by mixing analog with digital stuff.

Haslinger: There are two steps. You say, okay, an FM sound doesn't sound like a Minimoog. So you get a MIDI-to-CV interface and make it work. Then you find

out that against the other stuff, the Minimoog doesn't have the presence to cut through. It makes this warm bass sound, but it doesn't really appear. So the next step is to combine it with FM, which is what we're doing now. We have two basic analog units, the Minimoog and the [Roland] Jupiter-8. These are the two units that give something special.

Froese: It's so funny. Even big names in the business are shy about telling the public that they are still working with Minimoogs and Jupiter-8s. Most of them do, because it's a great sound.

But you do tend to acquire just about every major new instrument that comes out.

Haslinger: We're like little kids. Whenever a new piece comes in, we just grab it and eat it!

It can be overwhelming to have to learn continually how to use new musical tools. Sometimes it seems that it might be even harder to be familiar with the technology and to have to keep re-learning things than it would be to start fresh and learn from scratch.

Froese: Sorry, but I can't agree. If you know a bit about the general philosophy of electronics, the general ways of creating sounds, and what a tone really is, then if you want to create a new sound with the DX, you only have to know what a scaling curve is, how to set envelope rates, and so on. If you start really cold—if you love your acoustic piano and jump into a Mac or ST program—then you may get lost in the middle of a desert. I agree with you in the sense that once you realize what a computer really is, that a computer is machinery for a composer and never creates anything for which it was not programmed, then you can take away everything you've ever heard, kick away all of those song-type clichés, and start from a new ground. Then you really can start from your own imaginations of sounds. But you have to learn exactly what those machineries can do, and maybe even more important, what they can't do.

Do you make it a point to keep up? Do you consider yourselves avid students of the technology, or do you simply absorb what you need to?

Froese: To be honest, we are absorbing new knowledge like babies. We have been doing it for 20 years. When we get a new piece of equipment or software, we listen very carefully and then we talk to the designer. It happens from time to time that you sit in front of a technical genius, a person who has his head full of incredible ideas, and you have to bring him back down to earth. You have to say, "Look, a musician has to be able to make use of this. How can we make a philosophy which helps both of us?" You have to have a dream in your head, and maybe it can never be fulfilled, but it has to be there.

Haslinger: What most people haven't yet understood is that computers and high-tech equipment in music aren't anything more than a new form of instrument. If you sit down at a piano, you don't have to think about how it works. It is a very complicated process which goes from the key to the hammer to the string, but nobody cares. It's just a piano. You can sit in front of a piano and practice for eight hours a day and it's considered normal. If you sit down at a computer, everybody goes on about mathematics and all that, and nobody cares that it's an instrument that has to be practiced. You have to sit down and say, "This is my instrument, and now I just play." That's what we try to do very often. On the one hand, we're very interested in technical research; we're working with a lot of technicians, giving them our input. On the other hand, we've tried to set up our studios in a way that the keyboard and other controls are at the center, and can be played in a very musical way.

How is your studio laid out?

Haslinger: We rebuilt it so that the keyboard is placed in the center. All the acoustics and speaker systems are set up in such a way that the spot where you sit and compose will be the ideal place. And we pre-programmed a lot, so you can just sit and push buttons. When we do music, we do pure music. The time where we check out software and work with technicians is completely separate.

The fact that several instruments in the studio are only four or five months old must detract from the process you're describing. If you call up a sound that's close but not quite what you want, you're always tempted to stop playing and leaf through the manual.

Froese: That may be the most complicated point of all. We have the most up-to-date technology in our studio sometimes for three weeks, sometimes for three years. But we do not have the time to read through every manual. Sometimes it takes weeks before you understand everything. Our solution is to have a few technicians who read all the manuals for what we call the "daily equipment" and give us the key points. When we find an instrument that we fall in love with, and which lets you change the software so that it remains useful for at least a few years, then we go through all the facilities the instrument offers and work everything out for ourselves. I think the crucial point for most musicians on keyboards is that they have to spend a lot of time going through paperwork just to figure out that the instrument is exactly the opposite of what they wanted.

After all these years, Tangerine Dream must have an enormous library of sampled sounds.

Haslinger: We have a lot of storage in the back yard. But sampling is just another word for recording. The important thing isn't having the sounds, it's the context in which you're using them. With the 16-bit machines and the bigger storage capability, the time is not far off when we will have a junction of recording and instrument design. What we try to do already is when you sit there and play and compose, you have everything at hand—sounds, sequences, everything. You just need to store your ideas. Before long you'll be able to go direct to digital with everything. That's the idea behind the Synclavier, but that's still the wrong approach. If you want to make a musical movement in this world, you have to come up with a concept like a DX7, not a Synclavier.

Do you do new samples yourselves, or do you rely on things that you have in your archives?

Haslinger: We have one technician who just works

on samples. He comes up with sampling ideas, and we see what we can do with them. We need that a lot, because in film music work it's so important to have new, original sounds. On the other hand, we do adapt factory samples. Companies spend a fortune on good samples. Why not make use of them? With our sound devices we try to modify the sound until it's right.

How do you deal with the problem of organizing and accessing the sounds?

Froese: Just to name one instrument—not in the way of putting it above everything else—when we started working with the Emax Rack, we immediately saw that we needed some software to help us make perfect edits to the programs, and to work out the library. We worked very hard on that. Then we jumped around and started creating samples ourselves, and overlapping sampled sounds and digital sounds, and creating our own material. That can be done, I'd say, three times a year. Not more often, because we do not have the time to do it every month.

Haslinger: Thank God for the memory button! We always can press it whenever we find a good mixture of whatever instruments.

Froese: There are so many good drum sounds around, but unfortunately they're all on different instruments, so you can't dump them from one to the other. For some of our drum kit sounds, we use the Akai S900—for nothing else anymore. We use the Emax for some solo voices and some other sounds. All three of us have those instruments in our racks. Yet each of us has a personal way of looking at music. Someone may be more into the melodic area, another more in the rhythmic area, the third more in the harmonic area. So each of us has his very personal hardware setup where he feels familiar and comfortable.

How do these elements come together in the activity of composing?

Froese: We spent two years thinking very hard about how to do it, and we ended up talking over and over about the philosophy: What does it really mean to each of us to be a musician? Over the last year, we ended up just trading floppy disks, so that each of us can get familiar with the others' ideas. We have no excuses—we put on things that maybe the other ones don't like. In the end, we got together and figured out what one of us would do to the work another one has already done. This way, you see not just the pleasant side of the other person; you may see the side that can be very ugly, a side that you never thought of. Paul and I had worked together for two and a half years, and we

thought we knew each other. We played the sequences for each other and said, "Oh, sorry, who did that?" I did not know that something like this could come out of Paul, and maybe the other way around. To say it very simply, in a band like this we have to surprise each other. If we just do the same thing over and over, we lose our vitality.

Your music has changed over the years from spontaneous improvisations to fairly rigid compositions to, most recently, something in between, more like a patchwork.

Froese: You are right. We love the work we did because we could not do it any other way. It's totally crazy to complain about your kid just because it was born with two noses. What can you do about it? You have to love it because it is your kid. No one can say that you have to have the genius idea with every record you've ever composed. We are individuals and human beings. We are full of mistakes, and full of good ideas. The thing is to figure out when you are in a position to tell an interesting story. You'd better stay in bed when you're just in the mood for small talk.

When you discussed your philosophies as musicians, what came out of those conversations?

Froese: One night a couple of weeks ago, we figured out that music, what you hear as music, is maybe just ten or 20 percent. The rest is what you don't hear. Call it atmosphere, aura, the invisibility of the sound—everybody should find his own explanation for it—but the tone you hear is just a small percentage of what the music really is. When you sit down to compose and you hear the complete orchestration in your head, is it there for a person who sits beside you, or is it not there? I would say it is, and what you have in your head is even more important than what is created later using the instrument. It's a key point for our work at the moment to release more and more of that so-far unheard part of music, rather than just to create a new DX-whatever sound. It's something that you hardly can explain in words. As soon as a tone is there, it's gone, you know? How to grab it, how to keep it?

Haslinger: That's a very old story. Musicians have always struggled with it. But we are in a kind of new position, and we're not sure the usual way of seeing it wasn't a little short-sighted. They said, "We're going to put out music and that's it." They didn't think any further and say, "We create pictures, we create images, and we do care about how things will appear." What we're doing with our conceptions and compositions and philosophies is thinking about the picture, the appearance of what you do with your product. There are two ways of making music. One is to sit down alone in a room, close the door, and play the piano. That's an existential kind of thing—you do it with yourself. But if you decide to publish music, then our discussion starts. Because if you decide to give it to people, you should care a little more about how the appearance shows up. We know our creativity. We know we are workaholics—we work for 24 hours a day when we are into something—and it doesn't make sense to say, at a certain point, now it's finished. Publishing companies and others in the business don't care about it once the music is finished. But I don't think it's ever really finished. That's hard, but I think the way most musicians think of that point is probably too idealistic.

For an electronic group, Tangerine Dream is extraordinarily effective and experienced in a live situation. By this time, do you feel any limitations onstage, as opposed to in the studio?

Haslinger: Limitation is given by mind.

Froese: That's true. And it's becoming more and more true. The borders you think of are not actually there. There is no border as long as you do not start to think about borders. Every musician should think about that, as a general principle. The music world today could be much more different, and musicians could think about technology much more differently, if they would not build for themselves these borders. There are musicians I've spoken to, famous artists, who love computer music—better said, music created using computers—but they hate to start working with those instruments. By that fact, during interviews they start talking in a completely different way. They say, "What bullshit. I don't want to sit in front of a little screen during my creative process." People should start understanding that computers are nothing more than their little helpers. They are not geniuses. They are not the biggest thing on Earth. Absolutely not. They are just tools that help you to create things.

Haslinger: There are parallels in history. Every time a new instrument appears, there is first a period of exploring it. This was like when Tangerine Dream started, with the first synthesizers, the first steps into this new sound area. Now we've got to the second step, which is more about musical usage. It's not so much, "All right, we've got to check that out." It's more like, "What are we going to do with it?" □

A SELECTED TANGERINE DREAM DISCOGRAPHY/FILMOGRAPHY

Albums: *Alpha Centauri* (1971), Jive Electro (dist. by Relativity); *Phaedra* (1974), Virgin; *Rubycon* (1975), Virgin; *Stratosfear* (1976), Virgin; *Cyclone* (1978), Virgin; *Force Majeure* (1979), Virgin; *Tangram* (1980), Virgin; *Exit* (1981), Virgin; *White Eagle* (1982), Virgin; *Hyperborea* (1983), Virgin; *Le Parc* (1984), Jive Electro; *Underwater Sunlight* (1986), Jive Electro; *Tyger* (1987), Jive Electro; *Livemiles* (1988), Jive Electro (dist. by Caroline, 5 Crosby St., New York, NY 10013); *Optical Race* (1988), Private Music (dist. by RCA).

Film Soundtracks: *Sorcerer* (1977), MCA/Virgin; *Thief* (1980), Virgin; *Wavelength* (1983), Varese Sarabande (13006 Saticoy St., North Hollywood, CA 91605); *Risky Business* (1983), Virgin; *Flashpoint* (1984), EMI; *Firestarter* (1984), MCA; *Heartbreakers* (1985), Virgin; *Legend* (1986), MCA; *Three O'Clock High* (1987), Varese Sara-bande; *Near Dark* (1987), Varese Sarabande; *Shy People* (1987), Varese Sarabande.

Edgar Froese Solo Albums: *Aqua* (1974), *Epsilon In Malaysian Pale* (1975), *Macula Transfer* (1976), *Ages* (1978), *Stuntman* (1979), *Pinnacles* (1983)—all on Virgin.

ANDREAS VOLLENWEIDER

By Rick Gartner

Frets, January 1985

Cash registers are not his concern. This new age harpist from Zurich, Switzerland, is massaging audiences all around our planet with his sensual, pan-ethnic music—which just happens to have become a rousing commercial success. In three years he sold over a million records and achieved stardom in Europe. But that was unintentional. With Andreas Vollenweider, almost nothing is intentional. In fact, his music is about *avoiding* intention.

Improvisation is the wellspring of Vollenweider's soothing musical offerings. The engaging melodic motives and highly percussive textures that typify his work are born in the pre-dawn hours when the conscious world sleeps. It is at this time, when the artist is in the sublime state between sleep and consciousness, that he reaches for his harp and lets the music happen. *Later,* he writes it down—he never stops midstream to capture the moment.

The creative process matures through ensemble improvisation. The live performances of "Andreas Vollenweider And Friends" are essentially spontaneous, woven around a loose framework of musical substance and staging cues. Laying down the focal rhythmic grooves is a two-man rhythm section: drummer Walter Keiser, and multi-percussionist Pedro Haldemann, who taps, raps, and pounds everything from tuned wood blocks to Chinese gongs.

Center-stage is Budi Siebert, breathing life into a diverse array of wind instruments. Flutes and saxophones are his primary musical vehicles. He adds an occasional riff on accordion, and he also has an affinity for Andean pan-pipes, whose breathy sound embodies the spirit of this music. Keyboard synthesis is tastefully provided by Christoph Stiefel.

Andreas Vollenweider had his harp frame the right side of the stage setup. The instrument is a full-size concert harp (as opposed to the smaller Irish-style folk harp). Electronic reinforcement of the harp's mild amplitude is necessary, and the acoustic timbre is preserved through a built-in system that relies primarily on the output of both a microphone and a piezo-electric pickup for *each* string.

Other modifications include a personally tailored pedal system that can raise or lower the pitch of the strings by a semitone (half-step). That device is common on classical harps; but one of the ways Vollenweider utilizes it is rather ingenious. He achieves a legato effect very much like that of a hammer-on (or pull-off) by engaging the pedal after plucking a note during a melodic riff.

Vollenweider's harp also has a mechanism (activated by pushing a lever against his knee) that can "bend" notes by stretching the strings. Andreas made these (and other) mainframe modifications at home, in his own workshop. He also makes his own strings, although he can't tell you exactly how many it takes to fill out the extensive range (over six octaves) of his instrument. Since the harp is diatonically tuned (by scale steps, in the key of *C*), the string count is about 48. The strings are of various compositions, depending on the pitch.

Vollenweider follows traditional harp technique, in that he uses his left hand to cover the instrument's lower range. He wraps his thumb and middle finger with tape to protect them from injury, since they pluck the heavier-gauge metal bass strings. On his right hand, which plucks the treble stings, he has cultivated an incredible crop of fingernails—more like claws, actually. He keeps his left-hand fingernails short.

With the picking duties of each hand clearly defined (although there is occasional voice-crossing from hand to hand), his musical textures are often contrapuntal, although he does utilize arpeggios and other dramatic flourishes inherent to the harp. But he seems to take much more delight in finding ways to emphasize the percussive potential of his instrument.

Vollenweider's overall approach to harp technique is much like his approach to music. He goes by instinct, and he is very resourceful. That is also the case when he plays the *koto,* a Japanese zither, tuned pentatonically, with a movable bridge for each string. To

bend notes on the koto, he plucks a note with one hand, and reaches across the bridge with the other, pulling on the string to raise the pitch. His koto playing is unilinear, rather than contrapuntal.

While all his music is born through the spirit of improvisation, the musical detailing of Vollenweider's recording—unlike that of his live performances—is thoroughly worked out in advance. And on record, Andreas lays down the majority of the tracks himself. Harp, electric guitar, and some of the wind, percussion, and keyboard work is handled by the composer himself. He grew up in a home filled with musical instruments, and it shows. All of Andreas' supporting

tracks are tasteful and clean. And the production quality of the records is top-notch: beautifully mixed, and crystal clear.

There is no evidence of virtuosity, but that is not his intent. In fact, shows of virtuosity are purposely *avoided*, both on record and in concert. It's the mood and the balance he's after. Vollenweider wants to let the music be a bridge away from the material world to a transcendent, shared feeling of harmony. He feels that individual pyrotechnics are contrary to the spirit of his music, because such displays force the audience into the role of consumer, and he wants the people to be *participants*. This is not an excuse for musical

What's next? More of the same, one would hope. There are precious few *calming* influences shooting across the mediawaves these days.

* * * *

Your philosophy pays much attention to the metaphysical side of life—getting to "the space where the source of creativity is," as you put it. How does this affect your music?

What we are doing with our music—as are many other people around the world—is being aware of the medium we're using. The harp was—and still is for people in northern Africa—a kind of spiritual symbol. And most important, the harp has been the leading instrument to build a communication bridge between unconsciousness and consciousness. And you *need* another medium to make this communication flow. When the information gets from the unconscious mind to the conscious mind without being distorted, you can work with it; you can tap into that energy source. Music was initially created to be this space, this spiritual source. It has been that way in all cultures, since mankind has existed. But it became more and more superficial. Today this medium is being used instead mostly for entertaining. That is not enough. You have to *share* this process with others. This medium of music is a gift for us, and I do see in this country and all over the world many musicians who realize that this is a gift and that it shouldn't be wasted. We try to take the focus off ourselves, because the audience and the people onstage are all going through the same process. The only difference is that our hands are the physical objects that are touching the instruments. It is the *collective* energy which actually produces the music. And *that* is the main ingredient of our music. The collective energy comes from the outside to us, and it becomes alive through us.

Isn't it something of a risk to rely almost completely on improvisation for live performance?

The music is very simple so you can never get lost. If you feel as an individual in the band that you're lost you can go back to the basic structure, or you can just reduce what you're playing, and wait until you sense where the others are going.

Since the music is so structurally simple, how do you avoid becoming repetitious, or unspontaneous, when you play the same basic program night after night?

We have to surprise each other with little unexpected things so that the music stays alive. But this

mediocrity. All the members of the ensemble obviously are very accomplished, versatile players. And it is also quite apparent that they thoroughly enjoy every minute of their concerts. So do their audiences. Using the responses of critics and the public as a barometer, it's safe to say that there are a lot of Earthlings who will gladly part with a few trade units for a refreshing escape to Vollenweider's realm of space.

Such respected publications as Germany's *Audio* magazine have awarded his efforts with album-of-the-year honors (over the super-hyped music of Michael Jackson, and other American mega-stars). And yes, Andreas Vollenweider has made a video—*Pace Verde* (also an award-winner), which has been picked up by HBO, Showtime, and other cable systems. He not only produced and directed that project, but he also built all of the sets.

comes, as does all the music, from that shared space, that source of creativity. We can't rely on individual virtuosity—although each of us does have a certain amount of that—because as soon as the music would become ego-dynamic, the feeling and spirit of the music would be lost. There is plenty of virtuosic music around today, perhaps too much—and we don't want to become a part of that movement.

How do you feel about the general trends of music in contemporary media?

It's stuffing us, filling us up completely—most of the organized and unorganized noise that is around today. After being in this country for five weeks, the only real reason why I'm glad I can go back home—besides that I can see my family—is that it's *incredibly* noisy over here. As soon as you walk somewhere indoors, there is always music or television. There is no *silence*. And when you go outside, there is this absolute *terror* of noise in the streets. In Europe it's much quieter. We don't allow so many things to be so loud. For example, just this [the insistent hum of an air conditioner] would *kill* me if I had to listen to it all the time.

And it's almost impossible to get to that creative space in the midst of so much noise?

That's exactly right. I live in a very beautiful house, in a very beautiful place, but it's even getting difficult to find silence when I'm at home. I will probably have to move someplace else.

Back to more material concerns. You have quite an elaborate stage setup, with all the instruments and the electronic gear. You perform in very large, prestigious concert halls. How much of your equipment and stage crew do you carry with you on tour?

First, I always travel with all my own people, because they know the basic structure of the music, and they know when we're coming out of free improvisation back to the basic structure. They know what to do if there is a total change. Someone from the outside wouldn't ever be able to give us the right responses in the lighting, amplification, and so on. We bring almost all of the actual stage equipment with us from home, except the P.A. speakers and the lighting systems, which we rent when we get over here.

So once you actually begin the tour, you are carrying all of the equipment. How long does it take the crew to set up?

About four to five hours, depending on the situation. For example this hall [Davies Symphony Hall, in San Francisco, California] wasn't designed for amplified music with drums. We carry a lot of stuff to dampen the sound, to prevent feedback and so forth. Sometimes we have to virtually rebuild the hall.

At the end of the performance you made a very strong political statement. How would you say your music is tied to your politics.

Well, everything is political, really. Anything you do that involves people is political. There is an incredible feeling [in the world] of no tomorrow. Creativity has been sold out for material things and we are terribly out of balance. Music is one way to help re-establish the balance, and so in that way, what we are doing is political. For us that means providing a bridge of music for people to reach beyond the material world. □

A Selected Andreas Volleenweider
Discography
Solo albums (on Columbia): *Atmospheres*, (CD only), MXK-42313; *Behind The Garden*, FM-37793; *Caverna Magica*, FM-32827; *White Winds*, FM-39963; *Down To The Moon*, FM-42255.

GEORGE WINSTON

By Bob Doerschuk

Keyboard, January 1984

More than simply a piano player, George Winston is a phenomenon in contemporary American music. At first glance, he seems to be a throwback of sorts, evoking winsome shades of the hippie era. He could have stepped barefoot out of the Sixties, full beard, flowing pony tail (recently cropped), and all. His music is more of a paradox, though, touching on a broad range of pianistic influences that stretches back to old-timey stride players, leaps up to modern meditative minimalists, and, at least on the surface, skips over late-'60s rock untarnished.

It all adds up to this: Winston is ultimately a product of our times, and his music has achieved such remarkable renown because it serves the needs of a growing segment of the listening public. The question of where that need arose is one of the more beguiling mysteries confronting pop music demographers today. Winston's label, Windham Hill, was founded in the early '70s by guitarist William Ackerman, whose homespun style defined its direction. In ten years it has blossomed into a precedent-breaking success, wafting strains of soothing acoustic music through the electric logjam on the radio and in the record stores. Windham Hill's function may be characterized in part as that of an antidote for a jangled, perhaps nostalgic, community of ex-rockers, who find musical and even spiritual succor in the reassuring sounds of George Winston and the other Windham Hill artists.

At least in terms of sales, though, Winston is the biggest gun in this mellow melodic arsenal. *Autumn,* the first in his series of piano albums based on the cycle of seasons, has sold more than 400,000 copies since its release in November 1980, and continues its climb toward gold, while the two follow-ups, *Winter Into Spring,* released in May 1982, and *December,* out in November 1982, have enjoyed between 150,000 and 200,000 sales. By May 14, 1983, all three albums were high in the *Billboard* jazz charts—*December* at 5, *Autumn* at 9, and *Winter Into Spring* at 12.

Though Windham Hill signed a distribution deal with A&M Records late in 1983, most of these figures were reached without benefit of big-label distribution, the usual route that many smaller record companies take in order to get their products into as many stores as possible. Indeed, many of Winston's customers pick up his work in unorthodox places; though precise statistics are not available, a spokesperson for Windham Hill verifies that many of his albums have been sold through small book shops and health food stores—establishments that generally stock only one or two record bins and cater to people who want music to meditate or simply relax with.

Alongside Winston albums in these stores you may find an intriguing selection of names and albums: recordings made by jazz flutist Paul Horn in the Great Pyramid and the Taj Mahal, duets for saxophone and whale or wolf by Paul Winter, Rhodes improvisations by Steve Halpern based on colors and mandalas, Brian Eno's ambient series, Georgia Kelly's shimmering harp solos, mystical synthesizer pieces by Kitaro, Larkin's contemplative hymns on wood flute. Despite their many differences in style and sound, all these artists share a love of soft textures and silent spaces, and a tendency to take a static approach—without a sense of movement toward cadences or of operating within traditional structure, where verse leads to chorus, and free of the tensions that these cadences resolve. If new age music, the umbrella label under which this music is often categorized, can be saddled with any general descriptive traits, it might be these.

Once again, though, Winston doesn't quite fit the bill. His pieces work as well for massage and meditation as those of any new age player, in spite of certain elements he relies on that are seldom seen anywhere else in the genre. He too makes potent use of silence and sustained ringing tones, yet there is nothing mellow about his touch at the piano. In order to get the overtone splash he seeks in his long-held chords, he plays with a biting, bright attack that often brings out the piano's steely edge. He frequently uses a hypnotic ostinato in the left hand, or relies on pedal-point drones, but he always plays within an apparent, and rather traditional, structure. Winston's harmonies are never cluttered, and his voicings are stark. He has followed no trends within or without the new age movement; by borrowing from unexpected sources, he has staked out his own stylistic territory, and inspired other pianists to experiment along similar lines.

Perhaps Winston's simplicity, effective as it is, has an

overall negative effect. Perhaps young keyboardists feel that his approach offers them an excuse to cultivate no more technique than they need in order to emulate the pastoral power of his playing. If so, they miss the point. The key to George Winston's work isn't in his hands; it's in his ears, in the complex associations he makes between the many styles of music he loves, and most elusively, in his open-hearted approach to life.

Born in 1949 in Hart, Michigan, Winston has led a peripatetic life. He was raised in Miles City and Billings, Montana, and subsequently lived in Jackson, Mississippi, Miami and central Florida, Los Angeles, and, currently, in Santa Cruz, California. He began listening to music around 1960, being attracted at first to the country piano of Floyd Cramer and to the rock instrumental acts of the day—the Ventures, the Chantays, B. Bumble and the Stingers, the T-Bones, and others. After graduating from high school in 1967, he began playing in bands, this time following the bluesy footsteps of jazz organist Jimmy Smith.

He stayed with rock organ until hearing records of Fats Waller for the first time in 1971. The music was a revelation, inspiring him to abandon electronic keyboards at once and return to the piano. For a while he composed stride and blues pieces, many of which appear in his first album, *Piano Solos*, released originally on the Takoma label, but now available from Windham Hill under the title *Ballads And Blues: 1972*.

Winston remains a passionate lover of stride and early rock piano, but his experiments with slower, more reflective improvisatory work, also dating back to the early '70s, are what have come to dominate his style. Folk guitarist John Fahey was an early influence along this line, but the distinctive resonances of the piano itself provided the clearest path as he searched out his own mode of expression. Unfortunately, there weren't many opportunities for this kind of playing to be heard in the '70s, and George, discouraged, quit playing in 1977. Two years later, however, another enlightening album propelled him back into action: *New Orleans Piano* by the brilliant Louisianan Professor Longhair, a compilation of cuts recorded between 1949 and 1953. That, plus the good luck of making Ackerman's acquaintance, led to his affiliation with Windham Hill and his emergence as a unique and refreshing force in the piano world.

Winston's concerts are warm, intimate events. Whether appearing on college campuses or in Carnegie Hall, he approaches each performance with a disarming informality. He prefers playing barefoot and dressing in what might be called whole earth/casual fashion. During the first half of the program he plays various songs, some of them unreleased or borrowed from other artists; his rendition of Vince Guaraldi's "Linus And Lucy Theme" [from *Vince Guaraldi's Greatest Hits*, Fantasy, 4505] is a regular highlight. There are blues pieces, stride pieces, even an occasional solo harmonica workout. After the intermission, he turns to his albums on the cycle of seasons, playing work selected to match the time of year. Throughout the entire recital, he speaks to his listeners, treating them to a taste of his gentle humor, often extolling the many musicians whose contributions he gratefully acknowledges.

This list, by the way, is one of the most bewildering ever assembled. Winston's influences and musical heroes are many, their styles widely divergent. In the course of our interview, he cited the following names; Longhair, Guaraldi, de Grassi, Jimmy Smith, Jimmy McGriff ("I saw him on a TV show once doing 'I Got A Woman,'" Winston recalls. "He did the ending for about five minutes, and it was stunning. One of the most astounding pieces of music I ever heard"), jazz organist Gene Ludwig ("He had a swing, an expression, and a feeling for time. Oh, man Gene Ludwig, where are you?"), L.A. session player Artie Butler ("Remember that jungle piano on Joe Cocker's version of 'Feelin' Alright'? That got me into getting an electric Hohner"), Oscar Peterson, guitarist Bola Sete and Pierre Bensusan, harpist Andreas Vollenweider, Hawaiian slack-key guitarist Keola Beamer, Jon Lord ("I still listen to the organ solo in 'Hush' at least once a week"), a local jazz pianist in Miami Beach named Jim Casale, a musician in Palo Alto, California, named John Creger, whose slow tunes inspired him to study the music of John Fahey, Steve Reich ("They call him a minimalist, whereas to me, with all the complexities in his music, he's a maximalist"), Don Gallucci, who played organ with the Kingsmen of "Louie, Louie" fame, Brian Auger, Cleo Brown, Ralph Sutton, Dick Wellstood, two Los Angeles players named Brad Kay and Barry Gordon, Floyd Cramer, B. Bumble And The Stingers ("When I heard 'Nut Rocker' in 1962, that's the first time I ever said, 'Damn! That piano!'"), the Ventures ("I was real turned on by their organ breaks"), and many others.

Away from the keyboard, Winston is an eager conversationalist, whose energy overflow is channeled by his genuine modesty. He is a pacer, a gesticulator, brimming with an expressive restlessness that belies his introspective artistry at the piano. One of the only questions that slowed him down, during our conversation, was when he was asked how the recent unexpected surge in his income might affect his way of life over the next few years. He paused, thought for a few moments, and responded, "I don't really know. I've pretty much got what I want right now."

*　*　*　*

*U*nlike your albums, which seem to reflect a single specific mood from start to finish, your concerts switch in mood from one song to the next. Because your audience knows you largely through your more meditative material, don't you feel that there are certain styles, certain pieces, that you cannot play without thwarting their expectations?

No. A lot of that comes from my roots in playing music, which are different from my roots in listening to it. I started playing organ in rock bands in '67, and we'd always play two or three fast songs, then a slow one, throughout the night. I still have that same concept of breaking things up—three slow ones, one fast one, two slow ones, one fast one. I've never heard anyone say,"I wish you hadn't played that fast stuff." Duke Ellington said there are only two types of music—good and bad. For me, there are only two types of music I play—fast and slow. When I play a fast piece, I'm adapting to a part of myself that's more impish, and when I play the slow stuff it's more from the introspective side. Did you ever see that *Star Trek* where Captain Kirk went through the transporter and got split into two bodies? The mean half was killing himself by getting in trouble and making people want to get him, and the other half was so nice that he couldn't do anything. In the end, they both concluded that they needed each other to survive. That's the thing with me. If I was only doing slow songs, I'd be bored. If I was only doing fast ones, I'd need some introspection. I want to please myself as well as my audience. I want to do the pieces they know, like "Colors" or "Moon" [both from *Autumn*], but I also want to try new things.

That would explain why you shift from one style to the next so frequently in concert. But doesn't that make it much more difficult for you to create the kind of consistent flow of moods you achieve on records when playing onstage?

I don't think so. The songs from the albums are long; "Colors" goes anywhere from ten to as long as 18 minutes. I feel that's long enough. And that really sets people up for a fast number. They're not at home meditating; they're at a concert. I don't think people come to

the show in the same frame of mind as when they put on the *Autumn* record. I made those records for people who want to listen in their house, with one mood all the way through. When you go to a show, your adrenalin is up. You have to go through traffic, then you eat, and you get to your seat; that, plus, the conditioning that people have that they go to a show to get entertained, make it a different sort of experience.

What about concert programs themselves? How do you go about choosing the pieces and the order you present them in?

I make a set list about an hour before the show based on what I feel like playing that day. The sets certainly are oriented around the records. I play at least two or three things from each album, but I substitute other things a lot too. Stride kind of fits into the set because it's real entertaining. I can talk about Waller, and I do a bit of stride in "Colors" anyway. Ideally, the first half of the concert is made up of various tunes from the records, unrecorded things for harmonica, and so on, and the second set is centered around the seasons. That started happening last December ['82], when I played the whole *December* record for the second half. So the second half is really more like a record, but I'll also do other things related to the season, like Fats Waller's version of "Jingle Bells" [out of print]; it's a stride piece, not ambience stuff, but it's still winter.

Do you think the typical listener can make the identifications you intend in your music simply by hearing those pieces played? Could someone just pick up that your album Autumn *is about the fall season?*

I don't know. I don't want to sound overly humble, but the important thing about *Autumn* is that it's about the autumn, not that it's a piano record. It could have been a painting, or a guitar piece; it's the autumn idea that I'm really into. When I play "Moon," I don't say where the moon was when I wrote it, or if it's a cloudy night, or if you're just reflecting my own personal reality. It's not good to call it, "The Moon In Vermont On July 14," but it's also not good to say "Song No. 5."

You've mentioned your musical roots and how they underlie your approach to mixing a variety of styles in your concerts. Does your more reflective recorded persona also have ties to those same roots?

I think so, because what I'm doing now with the seasons albums is sort of impressionistic—it's music describing some idea or picture—and a lot of the music I listened to as a kid was impressionistic too. What I'm really doing is playing things like surf music, with the element of improvisation that I got out of jazz, and the element of improvisation in a very set style that I got out of blues. It's fun to play what's in your mind and your soul at that moment, but I need the structure; I can't create both the structure and the improvisation at once. And I need that impressionistic image. The first impressionistic piece I ever heard was "Powerhouse" by the Raymond Scott Quintet [out of print]. I used to put that on and fantasize adventures; I'd imagine a rocket ship speeding up. It was the same thing with "Pipeline" [by the Chantays, from *At The Hop*, MCA, AA-1111]. I didn't know that pipeline was a surf term, so I imagined some pipeline on the moon or in some ominous place. I call the stuff I do today impressionistic, too. They're mood pieces. I'm trying more to create an impression of something than to produce an absolute piece of music that somebody might want to transcribe or analyze. It's not like a piece by Bach that people arrange for harpsichord, organ, lute, guitar, or rock band. My pieces are not complete improvisations, but they're not completely set either.

Do you see your main musical strength as being in the realm of playing the piano?

I see my strength as an arranger. I think I play pretty well and I compose pretty well, but actually my main strength is as an arranger and entertainer. That's where my real self lies.

What's the most difficult thing about arranging your current pieces?

The thing I think about my stuff is that it's not that hard, but what is difficult is that since I play so diatonically, if I hit one note out of that scale, boy, does it stick out! A person playing in a more chromatic style can make almost any note fit in with what he's doing. But if I'm playing in *A* major and I hit a *B*, I just look at the audience and go, like, "Sorry," and they all laugh. I say, "Hey, let's just laugh at it. I don't like wrong notes any more than you do, but why have a bad taste in my soul about it forever?" It would be very nice to be able to play everything that's in my head, but I don't do that because I cannot spend all of my day sitting on a piano bench practicing when I've got these other musicians to produce and the guitar to play, and I've got to be on the phone.

When did you start developing an interest in the slower kind of improvisations we hear on your albums?

After I heard [folk guitarist] John Fahey in '71, I wanted to do slow tunes. I didn't want to play just the Fats Waller stuff anymore. I also tried to emulate [guitarist] Ry Cooder's phrasing, which is really fine, like [trumpeter] Louis Armstrong's. And Alex de Grassi was

a real inspiration. You know, I separate inspiration from influence; inspiration means, "Hey, I want to do my thing as well as he does his thing," and influence is, "Hey, I gotta get down with this guy's records and learn them all." Waller was an inspiration, and so were Professor Longhair and Vince Guaraldi. But I wanted to do songs like Alex'—with the same kinds of beautiful flowing lines. I wanted to do little Stephen Foster-type things that reminded me of winter or spring or something. I started wanting to go after sounds more than notes. If you hit the right combination of notes on a piano, the resonances really ring out. That's what really turned me on about playing the piano. Usually the key and chord changes of my songs are determined by how the resonances sound. I try to keep the sustain pedal down as long as I can. I do a song called "Untitled," where the pedal is down the whole time, which leaves time to let the notes die out. The sound I like most is the sound of overtones bouncing off each other. It's not an intellectual consideration; I'm not trying to be avant-garde or anything. I think I'm the opposite of avant-garde.

You say that you became more interested in sound than in notes themselves on the piano. Where did you find inspiration for this new focus?

After I quit playing in '77, I began listening to a lot of synthesizer players, like Klaus Schulze, Jean Michel Jarre, Michael Hoenig. I really liked the sound of those synthesizers. I guess I prefer playing acoustically, but when I started playing piano again, I wanted those sounds. I really have the feeling that the piano is an acoustic synthesizer. Now, when I play blues and stride, I don't think that at all; then I see the piano as a conga drum. But when I do the impressionistic stuff, I treat the piano like a synthesizer; I'm trying to find all the programs and sounds that it has.

Why were you not interested in doing these explorations on synthesizers?

Well, I really enjoy playing the guitar most of all, because I'm plucking the strings. The piano is pretty mechanical; all you do is change how hard you hit each note. But electronics are the same way. When I was playing organ in rock bands, I realized that I was always hitting the keys harder when I wanted to play harder. When I'd play a low chord, I'd tighten up my hand because the sound was so powerful. Maybe it's just a matter of getting used to any instrument, but I felt like my psychic or mental chemistry is better on acoustic instruments.

Are you interested in doing more recording on in-

struments other than the piano?

No, I just want to record on piano.

Why haven't you played your harmonica pieces on record?

I need to have some music that I just play when I feel like it, that's totally away from the business. If I don't record a certain harmonica piece, and then I decide to stop playing it live, nobody's going to say, "Why don't you play that harmonica thing anymore?" I play the guitar when I'm on the road, but I don't use it onstage. If I can play it whenever I want, and I don't have to play it when I don't want to, then it's more balanced to play the piano when I have to at a certain time each evening. It's not that I don't enjoy playing concerts. It's just that music is for me a spontaneous act, so if I can keep half of it spontaneous, then the non-spontaneous side is more fresh. I'm always looking for balance. I'm tending now to play shorter pieces anyway, because I've been editing some of my album things for release on 45 rpm singles.

Why?

To try to get a little airplay on adult contemporary stations. It isn't a compromising thing. I know there are musicians who feel that taking anything out of their stuff is a compromise, but to me it's an art form. I don't think I'm going to do any more ten-minute songs.

When did you get the idea of condensing your tunes down to single-release length?

After I did *Autumn* I got the idea of doing a single as a promotional tool. When I finally got a single done—"Colors," which was originally 10:25, and "Moon" were each cut down to about three minutes—and had it in my hand, it hit me: I had gone back to my roots, which are in AM rock instrumentals. It's not so important what your roots are, but when you go back to them, it's like, wow, an interesting realization. What I'm really trying to do with solo piano is what the Ventures did with "Walk, Don't Run." Just like they got instrumental rock on the radio, I'd like to get more solo acoustic music on the radio, so people can really hear the beauty of the piano out there. Why not have a nice three-minute piano record in between a couple of James Taylor or Joni Mitchell tunes? The version of "Blossom Meadow" from the *Winter Into Spring* album is three minutes, cut down from four, and I swear, I like the short one better. It's like the "Rain Sequence," from Will Ackerman's *It Takes A Year* [Windham Hill, 1003]. It's just a minute-thirty long, and then it's gone. I love that effect; it makes me want more. You don't get that from longer songs. I'd rather go with a little less than too much.

But if your intention on the seasonal albums is to paint a single consistent picture throughout the entire album, don't you lose that sense of development by slicing segments off in three-minute bits?

No, it's got to say the same thing. I'm still not thinking of singles in terms of money. It's more like, if I can get solo piano played on MOR or adult contemporary stations, then I'm accomplishing something, not for myself, but for solo acoustic music. I don't care if it's my music they play; if there's somebody else that gets played instead, more power to them.

How much of your impressionistic work is based on improvisations you've done, and how much is actually composed before recording?

It's a blend of the two, based on melodies I'd get in my head. Sometimes I get ideas by trying to learn somebody else's tune. For example, there's a very good unknown pianist in Hawaii named Paul Dondero. He had a tune that he said was inspired by Steve Reich and me, so I decided to learn it. By trying to learn his piece, I wound up making something that wasn't at all like it.

Do you do most of your writing at the piano?

Most everything I practice and mess around with at the piano I don't end up using, because the piano is not dead center for me. I'm always looking for that little dead center. Back in the '70s and in '80 or '81, when I was playing a lot more piano than I am now, I would think of a melody and have it on keyboard in my imagination; now I hear it on fretboard instead, although I usually play my ideas out on the piano first and then start playing them on guitar. Now, if I hear a lick in my head or in somebody else's music, I'm still going to learn it, but the main focus of my life now is on producing and guitar. I really like producing, because it lets me help people who have been making great music but have never recorded. Some of them look at recording as if it was like pulling teeth. It's not a comfortable thing for me either, but I've somehow been able to do it, and if I'm going to make records, I'd also like being able to help other people do it. So the piano is number three, which isn't bad; there are five hundred thousand other things I'm doing, and number three is still way up there. If the piano was number one, I might be a more versatile and accomplished player, but I think I'd also be getting stale.

Yet people see you primarily as a pianist. Will this be a hurdle for you to overcome in the future?

No, because I really love the piano. As long as I have an outlet for guitar, like playing it for a friend or making a tape for somebody, and for producing the musicians who've influenced me over the past 15 years, I'll be happy with the piano. I'm a better pianist than I am a guitarist, but the guitar really helps my piano playing.

Since you enjoy producing so much, why haven't you produced any of your own albums?

I'm simply not objective enough. My sessions aren't real long, but I like to get into the guts of a song and do eight or nine takes before peaking. I've got all the chords, I've got the rhythm, and the left-hand part is pretty set, but I don't know what the right hand is going to do, except that it's going to stay in whatever scale the song is written in. So I'll do eight or nine different improvisations, then take the one I like best. The left hand is kind of like a band, and the right hand is like the singer, and if the singer doesn't improvise a good scat, then, hey, he has to do it again. In classical music the two hands take an orchestral approach of working together like an ensemble, but I definitely take the band approach, and that means doing a lot of takes to get the right feel. By the time I've gotten through nine takes I need a little objectivity. I may have gotten into the groove of a song, but let's face it, a song is meant to be played just once. You don't play a song for a friend, then say, "Here, I'm gonna play it for you again." That doesn't happen in the real world. In producing other people, I'm learning to be me, not them. Sometimes when I'm producing I intentionally don't show up on time. This creates a mood like the teacher's out of the room or your parents are gone; for five minutes, you're free, and you can do whatever you want. That element of creating fresh is very important, because playing in a studio is an artificial thing. You are committing acoustic music through wires and electronics to a piece of vinyl. Lately I've learned to use the wire and the artificial process to make it sound more acoustic. It's like using a machine run by energy from petroleum to clean up an oil spill [*laughs*].

What led you to try this approach in recording the piano?

When I heard the Liz Story album [*Solid Colors*, Windham Hill, 1023], I said, "Oh, that's the sound I want for *December*. Same machine, same engineer, same piano." If it had been recorded on the moon, that's where I would have gone. It was like when I first heard the Doors with their Vox organ; that was it, the exact sound for me. Now, for *December*, I had this vision of pipe organs, because that's the time of year when people are celebrating. I was also starting to play in bigger halls when I made that record, so I wanted that sort of a sound, since ultimately what I'm trying to

do is make records that can be reproduced live.

Yet your studio effects, difficult to realize live, are what really gave the piano in December *its particular ambience.*

It was easy to reconcile myself to that, because the recording process itself is artificial, so why not do a few more artificial things to make the record sound like a piano really sounds?

What about the piano sound on your other records? Each album seems to have its own distinct one.

Well, on *Autumn* I didn't know anything, so we used the best techniques that Will Ackerman knew at the time. We used DBX with quarter-inch tape at 15 inches per second. On *Winter Into Spring* I used a Studer machine with half-inch tape at 30 ips. Now, January through March or April always seem stark to me, so I didn't use any added reverb on that album—only piano sustain. We did an interesting thing on *Winter Into Spring*, in the intro to "Venice Dreamer." I came up with the idea one night when I was sort of clowning around. I had my foot up on the low part of the keyboard and I played a scale with my right hand—the pedal wasn't down, but I was holding down the keys after playing them, so the notes really rang out. It was sort of like Columbus discovering America. So on the record I tried holding down the sustain pedal, hitting a chord with the right hand, lifting the hand off the keys and letting the pedal sustain the chord, but then raising the pedal up slowly to get that kind of buzz and cut-off effect where the dampers are half-touching the strings. But on top of that, there's this ringing that sounds like it comes from 500 feet away.

Was that because you had silently pressed the keys down again?

Yeah. So I used that on "Venice Dreamer," but I didn't want anyone to think it was a studio effect; it was part of the magic that the geniuses who invented the piano came up with. But it was also the nature of the album. It' not as joyous as *Autumn*; January and February are not as joyous as September and October, because people are waiting for the spring.

In spite of the differences in feeling and texture on your albums, and in a style between your work and that of the other Windham Hill pianists, is there any kind of common musical trait shared by the musicians on that label?

Windham Hill records represent Will Ackerman's musical taste. That's all. He chooses music that turns him on, so if there is a sound, it's his sound not mine or anybody else's. You could say that there was a Sun

Records sound back when Jerry Lee Lewis and Elvis Presley came along in the '50s, but that was [owner] Sam Phillips' taste. Elvis sounded different on RCA. I guess you could say that pianos do sound a little bit similar when there are more piano players around than guitar players or synthesizer players. You can get a lot more sounds out of a guitar or synthesizer than you can from a piano. And at Windham Hill the recording quality is definitely a top consideration.

Is it hard, then, to find a satisfactory live piano sound for your recordings?

It was in the beginning, but lately I've only been playing where I can get the sound I want. It's really silly of me to play someplace unless I can get the same sound I had on the record, because virtually everybody who comes to a concert comes because they have records, and they expect the same sound. It'd be like Jimmy Smith showing up at a concert with a Farfisa— not that Farfisa is a bad organ, but his recordings were made on a Hammond.

What kind of amplification do you use?

When I play big halls, I use the house P.A. I always tell the P.A. person to give me as little as he can: "Let's try nothing and go up." On a lot of that stuff, I hit notes and they linger out. The people in the middle or the back of the hall should be able to hear those, so the optimum for me is just a tiny bit, although it would be silly for half or a third of the house not to hear some of the notes just because I have an ideology of using as little electronics as possible. I'm probably going to start controlling that more by taking my own mikes around. I'm working with Tom Paddock, a great engineer from San Jose, California, who is really good at matching mikes, taking them apart, and perfecting them. I'll use whatever he recommends.

What about mike placement?

Usually what works best is having a couple of mikes, each one foot away from the bass and treble. I just leave it from there for the P.A. people, because they know their particular systems. It's hard for me to get out into the hall and listen to someone else play to check the sound, because I have a real personal way of touching the piano. But I do try to have somebody hit a few chords and let them linger, then I'll listen to P.A. hiss or something like that.

What pianos do you most enjoy playing on?

I really love Steinways. Sometimes the top part is real soft. Sometimes you get more of an average top, with a good mid-range or a real deep bass. I've never found one that was perfect, but that's probably like looking for the perfect car; there are too many variables. Yamahas are my second favorite. I do like the Steinway sound a bit better, but I would certainly never complain about having to play a Yamaha.

What do you especially like about the Yamahas?

When I was doing *Winter Into Spring* I wanted to get a harp-like tone. I asked a tuner what to do, and he showed me a screw on the right side of the keyboard on the block that you can tighten to make the action slide over further than normal when you press down the damper pedal, so that the hammers strike just one string instead of two. This lets you get extremely soft in a particularly tender passage, and gives you a chance to work with a wider range of dynamics. The only problem is that you can accidentally brush the hammer against the left strings of the neighboring notes if you push the action too far over. To take care of that, I block off the leftmost two strings with one of those rubber mutes that tuners use. This gives you only one string available per note, but that's the breaks. On "Carol Of The Bells" in *December* I blocked off two to three strings in the whole upper range, which gave me a really nice little bell sound.

If you've muted those strings, why alter the action position at all? You could just deaden most of the strings that way.

But I like the low notes, which just have one string per note, to be softer too. Plus I have a choice of pushing the pedal halfway down or finding other nuances.

Do you ever play the strings inside the piano directly?

I really don't like the sound of strumming on the strings that much, but if I want to get harmonics like guitar players do, I might put my hand on the strings to mute them, then lift if off a little bit. There was a tune called "Night Suite" on *December* where I marked the strings in the *A* minor scale, then played them individually up near the bridge like I would play my guitar, using certain parts of the nail or the flesh. And sometimes on "Colors," where I play a slow left-hand thing in the beginning, if the notes are ringing long enough, I can hit a note with the right hand, mute it real fast with the left, then shift my left hand back down to the keyboard on the beat. That gives the same kind of tension to the note you hit with your right hand that a guitar player gets when he mutes a note; a ring seems to come out of nowhere, and the reverberation is almost louder than the note itself. I also enjoy plucking or hitting the strings with the soft pedal on; that makes them hard and soft at the same time. You can get a brightness

without the brash percussivness that sometimes knocks people out of their seats. You can also hit a chord at the end of a song, but then put your fingers on some other keys and hold a different chord without actually playing it. As you gradually clear the sustain pedal, you end up with this unexpected chord that came out of nowhere. That stuff turns me on. At the end of "Some Children See Him" [from *December*], I found these little trumpet sounds on the piano that way, which was great because Alfred Berg, who composed that song, was a trumpet player. Most pianists let up on the pedal when they hear that buzz. Well, I'm looking at how far I can go with it.

You often seem to pursue a tranquil, even meditative, musical effect through the use of a very hard and percussive attack. What led you to try combining these seemingly contradictory elements?

That came from when I used to live in an apartment in Los Angeles. The neighbors were nearby, so I would play with the mute on and experiment with using a hard attack to get all these soft ambient tones. But I think there are a lot of other great players who are more into the meditation field than I am. If it happens, it's because of the piece; the song dictates it. I'm not trying to get it, or do new age or healing music. I've never tried to have a song be meditative on purpose. If that's the way someone reacts to it, fine. If they want to run around the block instead, that's fine too. I do a lot of slow stuff, but only because that's how the stars or the moon at night make me feel.

In your impressionistic approach to making music, you seem to identify more with painters than with people who practice spiritual exercises.

Yeah, but one thing about music and art is that part of it is an attempt to express something spiritual in the material world so people can experience it. By the time it gets to that point, it's not exactly the same thing you first imagined, but if it represents the sum total of what I felt, then I've done my job. You can dream of doing something, being a great baseball player or whatever, then when it comes time to do it, you might discover you're not quite that good. It's a rough world. What gets me through it is that I view it as a training ground or an obstacle course that I can learn a lot from. Otherwise it would have overwhelmed me a long time ago.

Do you find it easier to deal with that obstacle course while playing music? Is that one reason why you came out of your brief retirement in the '70s?

No, not really. In fact, I don't feel any different as a person when not playing music, because in both times I'm still dealing with feelings, dreaming of things, and wanting to do things. My obsession changed from basketball to playing the organ in 1967. I personally didn't feel any different; I just thought I'd use a different medium. I was also trying to eliminate the competitive thing. Some people like to think that musicians compete, but I consider myself totally non-competitive. Competition in music is a constructive thing when you're just beginning to play, and you want to play faster than the person down the block, so you practice a lot, but there's a point where that should stop and technique becomes a tool rather than the center of your music.

Why did you quit playing?

I had been studying a lot of music when I quit— music from India, Arabic stuff, Irish stuff, solo guitar stuff I was trying to convert to piano—but I realized when I heard Waller that his style was really where I was at. It was almost as if I had played stride in some kind of past life period. You know how sometimes you read a science fiction book that gets you so excited that you literally blow a fuse and just go to sleep? Or when you hear a record that's just too good, so you have to put it aside for a while? I think that's what happened with stride piano.

Are you saying that Fats Waller's excellence was a catalyst in your decision to withdraw from the scene for a while?

Yeah. It wasn't a conscious decision to take a rest; it was more like, "I'm tired of this, and I've gotten all I can out of it. I'm not going to do it anymore." It was like fasting, and it was the best thing I could have done. To me, Waller is just as complex as Bud Powell or Art Tatum; every time I hear him, I hear something new. Working out his more complicated things was hard, but trying to get his sound and feel was even harder. He had such delicacy and power; most of us mortals can only do one of those. Fats was like Jerry Lee Lewis in that it wasn't just the piano or what he was playing; it was his being. With Fats it was the impishness behind what he did; it just made you want to giggle, where Jerry Lee Lewis makes you want to yell and scream. I could name a lot of great Waller pieces—"Valentine Stomp," "Handful Of Keys," "Russian Fantasy"—but when I heard "Brand New Suit" [from *Complete Fats Waller*, RCA, AXM2-5583], that was the killer. I finally had to face the fact that I was never going to reach Fats. It was a nice try and a wonderful goal, but it was hurting my playing because it was making me want to give up. I mean, I've never heard Fats hit a wrong bass note.

You don't think you could have brought your technique up to his standard through diligent practice?

Well, I'm not a virtuoso in any way, but even if I was, I probably wouldn't play too differently from how I play now. What I lack in technique, I think I have in balance, and for me to get superior technique would upset that balance of what I'm doing as a producer and the other things I mentioned before. I've got to play some to maintain what technique I have, but if I play too much it defeats the whole purpose.

Do you do any practicing at all these days?

I don't get the chance, so to make up for that I've put those little weights that tuners use to hold down keys into the action on my upright, to make the action tougher at home than in the concert hall. I wouldn't recommend doing too much of that; a runner trains with leg weights on, but you don't want to run with hundreds of pounds strapped to your legs. I just wanted to make the action a little bit stiffer than what I'd run into on the road, so what practicing I can do at home is more worthwhile.

How do you warm up for a concert?

I stretch and do hand exercises. I warm up on the harmonica and the guitar. I generally find that it's a little better if my mind is active instead of trying to meditate or getting real calm. That way I can focus on the reality of how I love the audience, rather than think, "God, I'd rather go home." That's only fair to the audience. They're not there to deal with my problems; they want to hear some things they've heard before, and a few surprises. I can tell you one thing: I don't mean this to be derogatory, but it's simply a fact that the music business takes from music without giving back. What gives music back to me is life: just seeing the trees in Vermont, or being at home, or seeing some hummingbirds. If I was going to start writing songs about an auditorium or a hotel or a cab or being on the road, I'd have dead music.

Do you think you might once again go through a withdrawal from performance similar to the sabbatical you took in the '70s?

One can never know, but I imagine that at some point there'll be a rest of some kind. I'm definitely open to the idea. I think that for a musician to feel like not playing and to decide not to play is just as fulfilling and just as much a part of the growing process as feeling like practicing all day long. It's not a negative thing at all. In fact, when I started playing again, I played only the deepest things that I felt, instead of a lot of music I had only kind of wished I could have played. It helped me separate myself as a listener and player.

What kind of separation is that?

As a listener and a player, I'm like two very different people. As a listener and recording artist, I'm the same.

I tend to like an hour or two of similar moods of music, so my habits as a listener are reflected in what I do on the records. The period of not playing really helped me realize that just because something turns me on, that doesn't really mean that deep down I want to play it. Now, the only songs of mine that I do are the ones that are really at dead center for me, that say it really clear.

Do you have any interest in moving beyond the solo piano format into ensemble playing?

No, I don't hear that in my head. That's not in my dead center. I'm not against it, but I just don't anticipate doing anything like that. Plus I think it's so special when you hear a good solo instrumentalist. I remember seeing Jose Feliciano and his guitar; it was my first exposure to solo guitar, and it was like, "God! No band! Wow!" I got so turned on I decided to get it going all by myself too. Meanwhile, the bass player had quit my band, so I started playing a Fender bass keyboard with the electric piano, turning the bass all the way up. Then I started playing all by myself, not at gigs, but just for fun. I don't arrange any of my stuff for ensemble nowadays, but sometimes somebody else may ask me to do the kind of piano playing I do well for something they're writing—simple, ambient stuff. If it fits and I like it, sure, we'll put it on the record, and I'll play with it live once a month, but that's always somebody else's project. Lots of times I'll recommend some other piano player who's maybe not as well known as I am, but who would do a better job for that record. Anyway, people don't come up to me like that all the time. Playing solo piano kind of keeps you from the kind of wierd adulation where people idolize you. They show up to listen because they like the music; it's not a hype thing at all. That's another reason why solo is kind of good; no matter how big the audience, it's not going to treat you like a famous rock band. It's simply that I respect the audience and they respect me.

That's interesting, because you've played some very effective duets with Will Ackerman.

Oh, he and I are very close in style and taste. He has a beautiful style, very ambient and basic.

You seem to play more two-handed chordal passages, as opposed to the left-hand ostinato style you have when playing solo.

Yeah. I'm merely complementing what he's doing with two-handed voicings. Coming from music like blues, I'm used to keeping a rhythm going. The classical approach means using your two hands as one. In fact, Liz Story has a nice thing where she'll have two hands doing one thing, but my approach is more primitive: The left hand gets its thing down, like in boogie woogie, and then the right hand gets freer and freer. The left hand stays below Middle *C,* and the right hand stays above. It's like the left hand is the band, with the bass, drums, and rhythm section, while the right hand is like the singer. I never know what the right hand is going to do. There's a certain head [theme] and melody, but when I go into the studio I choose the take that has the best right-hand improvisation. I'll memorize what it does, play it kind of like that in concert, and take off from there. It's funny. The right hand is really like a singer; it gets all the credit.

Well, that's where the melody usually is, and people can relate easily to that.

But my whole thing in piano and guitar is the left hand. I ask myself, "What is the left hand setting up?" It really does all the work.

You've talked extensively about your influences, but what kind of impact do you feel you have made on today's pianists?

Well, I don't feel like anybody is copying me.

Judging from some of the albums that are out now, your influence is quite strong.

I don't know, it might just be a coincidence.

I don't think so.

Well, maybe it's like when Keith Jarrett had a hit with the two-record set from his Koln concert [*Koln Concert,* ECM, 2-1064-65]. A lot of jazz players responded to it, but I don't think they were influenced by him as much as they were encouraged by the success he had, and the record companies as well were encouraged to put out solo piano records once more. There are players who probably thought, "I have one solo piano record in me. Why not do it?" Maybe my records made even more of them think the same thing. John Fahey's guitar records encouraged me the same way. I was playing solo piano before I heard Fahey, but Fahey's music made me think, "Hey, I'm playing piano sort of the way he plays guitar. Why shouldn't I try making albums too?" Maybe that thing is happening again with my records. If that's true, fine. If that's what turns somebody on, more power to them. Music is available to everybody, that's for sure. □

A Selected George Winston Discography
Solo albums (on Windham Hill): *Autumn,* 1012; *Winter Into Spring,* 1019; *December,* 1025; *Ballads And Blues,* 0081; *Country,* 1039.

YANNI

By Bob Doerschuk

Perhaps in a former life he sailed with Ulysses, surviving adventure after adventure before struggling back to Greece and memorializing the whole thing in deathless verse. Travel is easier nowadays, but the spirit of romance lives on. So rather than risk his neck with sirens and cyclopses, Yanni takes his trips within, and uses his keyboards to tell us where he's been.

On his first two albums, *Keys To Imagination* and *Out Of Silence* , the Greek-born synthesist offered concise but vividly orchestrated instrumentals. Though they were quickly slotted into new age bins, their prominent melodies and often propulsive rhythms encouraged listeners to move rather than meditate. In particular, Yanni's plucked-string timbres and folk-like themes seemed to echo songs sung by ancient balladeers in distant mythic lands.

Never mind the fact that Yanni lives now in Los Angeles. Or that his most recent undertakings were two soundtracks set much closer to home than Troy or Homeric Greece. When he goes to work, he lets his mind wander far afield, free from the confines of his studio. "I'm not the type of person who just sits at the keyboard and plays for no reason whatsoever, then accidentally stumbles across a line that he can turn into a song," he insists. "I have to visualize things first, so I go to great lengths to get the mood in the studio just right. I'll bring in candlelight, or even a glass of wine if I need to. Sometimes the lights will be totally out. I'll create a daydream. Once I can imagine I'm there, so that I can even smell the place, I can begin."

For *Out Of Silence*, Yanni drew heavily on his return to Kalamata, the small Mediterranean town where he was born with the name Yanni Chryssomallis 33 years ago. He had left for the States at age 18 to study psychology at the University of Minnesota, going back for the first time 13 years later. "I wrote a lot of the album while I was there, in my own shorthand on little pieces of paper," he remembers. "When I got back to the States, I went straight into the studio, and stayed there for four months. I didn't come out until everything was written."

Keyboard, May 1988

This visual approach to music helps Yanni on his other projects as well, from his solo piano contributions to *Piano Two* to soundtrack work. The fact that the piano was Yanni's first instrument helped him practice on his Schaffer & Son grand for *Piano Two*, but he had also practiced scoring movies as a hobby in years past. "In the old days, I was so interested in soundtracks that when I saw a movie I loved that had music I didn't love so much, I would take a copy of the film home, recut it, and write a new soundtrack for it," he says. "I've done 50 or 60 films that way. Now finally, I get to do this for real."

The first Yanni score was for a TV film titled *Nitti*. Based on the life of Frank Nitti, Al Capone's right-hand man, it called upon Yanni to reflect the show's mix of darkness and sentimentality. "I didn't do it as a gangster move," he insists. "I did it as the story of a human being who came over from the Old Country to make a living, so the music is very acoustic. I played accordion and piano, and I hired people to play saxophone and clarinet, mandolin, and violin. The acoustic piano is blended with electronic piano, the violin with electronic strings, but when you listen to it, you don't know that it's electronic. The tone is very Italian, which is great because that gets me away from what I do on most of my albums."

The second soundtrack was for *Heart Of Midnight*, an upcoming feature film that Yanni describes as "a psychological thriller. Unlike *Nitti*, it required extremely electronic sound. The director, Matthew Chapman, did ask me not to do the kind of screechy violins you typically hear with suspense films. So I tried to accentuate the negative aspects of human nature. Again, it's totally different from what I do on my albums."

Yanni's method of translating his experiences into music is more impulsive than methodical. Though his deftness as a programmer is obvious, he fears that any analysis of how he puts his sounds together misses the point. "It's like going up to Steven Spielberg and say-

ing, 'I watched *E.T.*, man. What a great movie! By the way, remember that third scene ten minutes into the film? What kind of lens did you shoot that with?' Who really cares?"

Not that Yanni is oblivious to the intricacies of music technology. Far from it. In fact, he makes it a point to study each synth and sampler in his collection thoroughly, with owner's manual in hand. The point, however, is to become so familiar with his instruments that he learns to use them instinctively. "Have you ever been around a whiz kid while he's working at a computer terminal?" he asks. "He can program and talk to you at the same time, and you're amazed. That's how I feel around my keyboards. I don't go, 'Let's see. Which envelope should I use?' I just do it."

When pressed on how he constructs his trademark sounds, such as the bouzouki timbres on *Out Of Silence*, he says, "I usually do my plucked sounds on about four MIDIed keyboards. This makes it easier to do correct timbre changes. When I hit the key a little harder, it sounds like I'm pulling the string; maybe it buzzes a little bit. On a song like 'Acroyali' [from *Out Of Silence*] I also played the way a Greek *tamimi*, or free-form bouzouki player, would play. First I'll look toward my DXs, because their algorithms are good at giving a pretty sharp attack. For long milky sounds, I may look toward my [Sequential] Prophet-VS and the [Ensoniq] Mirage or [E-mu] Emulator. So I do have basic attitudes toward the instruments. But," he cautions, "I don't want to get into that."

Despite his reticence to explore programming specifics, Yanni rhapsodizes over the timbral doors opened by music technology in general. "When I got my first synthesizers, it dawned on me that until now every composer had much more limited resources," he says. "There were cellos, violins, horns, drums. A hundred sounds? Two hundred? Even a thousand? Big deal. Yet sound is half of music, the other half being composition. In the past, composers differed from one another only in their compositional skills. Now, all of a sudden, here are a hundred million sounds, a hundred million colors to paint with. Ten-year-old kids know how to use computers now, and soon they'll be going to school and studying music. They'll have all these sounds at home, and all these great ideas. And guess what? They'll be able to get them across. There's going to be a lot of little Yannis out there."

For now, there's only one, and you'll be hearing more from him soon. In addition to the TV and film work, he is finishing up another album for late 1988 release. Perhaps this variety of activities will eventually free Yanni from being perceived as a new age artist. If not, however, he doesn't mind.

"When I was studying psychology, I learned that one of the worst things you can do to patients is to label them," he remembers. "If you call someone a neurotic, he'll go into his box and behave like a neurotic. But we have to use labels, because they help us to communicate quickly and understand each other. That's why the new age label doesn't bother me. I can tell people I'm in that section of the record stores, and they'll find my music. See, I want my music to be heard. I want it to affect people. I want to connect with my audience at an intimate level. The best compliments I've ever received were when somebody called me and said, 'I was listening to your album last night, and this one song made me cry.' That's when I know I'm getting through. I don't want to be wallpaper. I don't want anybody to think that you have to be a spacehead to enjoy my music. If I can affect you emotionally and get under your skin, I'm succeeding." □

A Selected Yanni Discography
Solo albums (on Private Music): *Keys To Imagination*, 2008; *Out Of Silence*, 2024. *Optimystique*, Varese/Sarabande (13006 Saticoy St., Hollywood, CA 91605), STV-81215. **With others** (on Private Music): *Piano Two*, 2027; *World Of Private Music Sampler*, 2009-1-P9.

DENNY ZEITLIN

By Bob Doerschuk

Keyboard, October 1988

Leaning back in his chair, with the undulant hills and soaring skyline of San Francisco gleaming in brilliant sunlight outside his office window, Dennis J. Zeitlin, M.D., loosens his tie, clears his throat, and explains why one of the world's foremost jazz pianists—Denny Zeitlin—recently decided to test the new age waters.

"Paul Winter approached me with an interesting challenge," recalls Zeitlin, whose parallel careers in music and psychiatry seem about as big a challenge as any mortal could handle. "Would I be willing to record an album that would represent the most lyrical and simple aspects of my music? Paul had been following my music for years, and even though his personal bent is toward simpler forms, he's always liked my more complex style. But in terms of what he was attempting to do with his new label, Living Music, he wondered whether I would consider working in a more limited area, while trying to make it as beautiful as I could."

Intrigued, Zeitlin accepted Winter's invitation. In many ways, it seemed too interesting a possibility to pass by. Winter, considered by many a forerunner of new age music through his work with the Paul Winter Consort, started out as a jazz saxophonist, and therefore has a healthy respect for his longtime friend's talents, which are exhibited on a long string of albums stretching back to the mid-'60s. And Zeitlin, who has lectured and written extensively on the mysteries of improvisation, sensed that working with Winter could yield interesting insights into a style toward which he harbored decidedly mixed feelings.

"Paul never used the words 'new age' to describe what we were doing," Zeitlin says. "I know he doesn't like that designation. Still, I'd say that some of the earliest music that I would put under that banner came from Paul. Much of what he does at least typifies an area of that genre that I really enjoy a lot, in which artists who are not easily classifiable as rock or jazz or classical or anything else integrate a lot of different musical forms and play it all very well. This music can be soothing, but it's also challenging. I think it's terrific."

But other aspects of new age music leave Zeitlin less than enamored. "For me, at least, some of it is appallingly banal, horribly performed, and seemingly aimed at the lowest common denominator of human perception or tolerance of nuance. I can't really stand this approach. It's hard to find common ground between this and the sort of work that Oregon or Paul's Consort do. You can't say it's all meditative music, or music designed to soothe, or that it has very simple harmonic constructs. That's true of some of the music, but not all of it. One thing you can say is that it's not easily classifiable. To some degree, it's kind of a waste-basket category."

And so Zeitlin disappeared into his home studio with a Steinway B grand piano, Winter at the Nakamichi F-1 console, and more than a few apprehensions. "My goal was to come out with music that could simultaneously function in two ways," he says. "It could be ambience. You wouldn't have to pay attention to it as it played. There wouldn't be a lot of things that would grab you and *make* you listen. At the same time, I was hoping that if somebody cared to listen, they would find other levels of musical richness. I was worried, though, that I might be embarrassed about getting into some of these forms, that it would feel inauthentic or unmusical, or that it would be so far from me that I couldn't embrace it."

After a while, Zeitlin and Winter came up with *Homecoming* [Living Music (dist. by A&M), 998], a collection of solo piano improvisations. Though impeccable technique, restrained jazzy voicings, and introspective melodic extemporization seem to combine nicely in Zeitlin's hands, the marriage of styles and philosophies represented on the record was not as effortless as it sounds.

"Throughout the whole thing Paul was, in essence, saying, 'Simpler! Shorter! Terser! *Easier!,*'" Zeitlin laughs. "And I was saying, 'Man, there's only so much evisceration this music can tolerate!' We had to go back and forth, and try to find tunes that we both wanted to use. As it turned out, that really was't the easiest task in the world."

Ironically, it was Winter who helped steer *Homecoming* from the extreme simplicity that Zeitlin had expected to pursue. "I was willing to exist without any angularity or edge or fast tempos for the whole album," the pianist remembers, "but because Paul's way of working is an evolution of his own feelings and tastes, he shifted gears midway through and decided to include a few up-tempo tunes. And although I was also trying to avoid the kinds of structures that typify American popular music, Paul asked me to include 'Quiet Now,' which I had written with a standard A-A-B-A form."

Zeitlin is satisfied with his performance on *Homecoming*, yet many of his reservations about new age linger. "Steve Halpern and other people consciously set out to get sounds together that would reduce psychological stress, and that's very useful," he concedes. "What worries me is that this aspect of the music is spreading, almost like a disease, throughout the population, so that people might have less and less tolerance for music that demands something of them. Some people like to put on earphones and listen to 30 minutes of the Pacific Ocean. If it works for them, I have no quarrel with it. But I am not comfortable with the fact that there's less room in the marketplace for music that has a tremendous personal point of view, that invites—if not demands—that the audience wrestle with it. From that kind of interaction, a real soul-soaring experience can occur, as opposed to a soul-soothing experience."

Why don't more people seek the potential for ecstasy that lies beyond the frontiers of new age? "A lot of people avoid challenging situations, whether in interpersonal exchanges or in music," Zeitlin notes, "because of all kinds of internal fears, prohibitions, and conflicts. When these get resolved, people are generally more open to a wider variety of experiences, making it more likely that somebody coming home from a hard day's work might let some challenging music take them on a different sort of trip, rather than listen to a *C* major chord reiterate for half an hour."

Maybe *Homecoming* will be a first step in this direction for restless new agers. Then again, maybe not. "I was surprised to learn that Dick Conti is using *Homecoming* as background music for his show at KCSM," Zeitlin chuckles. "That tickles me. I never thought that any of my music would be used specifically as background music." □

About The Authors

Jim Aikin is an associate editor for *Keyboard* magazine. He has been with them since 1975 and has written many important features and articles on synthesizer art, performance, and technology.

Jeff Burger is a freelance writer based in southern California.

Bob Doerschuk is an associate editor for *Keyboard* magazine, and has been on its staff since 1977.

Dan Forte is an editor at large for *Guitar Player* magazine.

Freff is a well-known music journalist and *Keyboard* magazine columnist.

Rick Gartner is a former assistant editor for *Frets* magazine.

Ted Greenwald is a Windham Hill Recording artist, and a former assistant editor for *Keyboard* magazine.

Mark Hanson has authored two music technique books, and is an assistant editor for *Frets* magazine.

Phil Hood is the editor of *Frets* magazine.

Tom Mulhern is the senior associate editor of *Guitar Player* magazine.

Dominic Milano is the editor of *Keyboard* magazine, as well as an active performer, programmer, and design consultant.

Elisa Welch Mulvaney is a performer of Celtic (Irish) music, and an assistant editor for *Frets* magazine.

From GPI Books

SYNTHESIZER BASICS (Revised)

A valuable collection of articles from the pages of *Keyboard* magazine covering all facets of electronic music. Includes chapters on: perspectives on synthesizers, understanding synthesis, MIDI, sound systems and components, and recording electronic music. Also included are hardware and software manufacturers' addresses, recommended books, and a complete glossary. Contributors include: Helen Casabona, Ted Greenwald, Bryan Lanser, Dominic Milano, Bob Moog, Bobby Nathan, Tom Rhea, and the staff of *Keyboard* magazine.
ISBN 0-88188-552-5 $14.95   From Hal Leonard Publishing.

SYNTHESIZERS AND COMPUTERS (Revised)

A comprehensive overview, useful for beginners or seasoned pros, or anyone interested in the future of music. Includes discussions of digital audio, synthesis, sampling, MIDI, choosing software and interface hardware, and choosing the right computer. Also included is a section on Programming Your Own Software—which leads the reader step-by-step into the world of writing music software, and covers many insider's programming tips. From the pages of *Keyboard* magazine, with articles by Steve DeFuria, Dominic Milano, Jim Aikin, Ted Greenwald, Jim Cooper, Bob Moog, Craig Anderton, and other leading experts.
ISBN: 0-88188-716-1 $14.95   From Hal Leonard Publishing.

SYNTHESIZER PROGRAMMING

Don't be satisfied with factory presets! Get the most out of your instrument, whether it's a battered Minimoog or the latest digital dream machine. You can create your own unique sound with the concrete and understandable information in this practical introduction to programming and synthesis. With contributions by Wendy Carlos, Bob Tomlyn, and the editors and staff of *Keyboard* magazine. Includes specific guidelines for the DX7, Oberheim Xpander, CZ-101, Roland JX8P, and JX10.
ISBN 0-88188-550-9 $14.95   From Hal Leonard Publishing.

SYNTHESIZER TECHNIQUE (Revised)

How to utilize all the technical and creative potential of today's synthesizers, with discussions of Recreating Timbre, Pitch-Bending, Modulation and Expression; Lead Synthesizer; Soloing and Orchestration. Hands-on practical advice and instruction by leading practioners, including Bob Moog, Tom Coster, George Duke, Roger Powell, and others. Diagrams, illustrations, and musical examples throughout. Edited from the pages of *Keyboard* magazine.
ISBN 0-88188-290-9 $14.95   From Hal Leonard Publishing.

MULTI-TRACK RECORDING

Information on the latest home and studio recording techniques and equipment, edited from the pages of *Keyboard* magazine. Includes chapters of Getting Started, Outboard Gear, Synchronization, Keyboard Recording, and Advanced Techniques And Technical Change. With contributions by Bobby Nathan, Bryan Lanser, Dave Frederick, and the staff of *Keyboard* magazine.
ISBN 0-88188-552-5 $14.95   From Hal Leonard Publishing.

THE ART OF ELECTRONIC MUSIC

The creative and technical development of an authenic musical revolution, from the Theremin Electrical Symphony to today's most advanced synthesizers. Scientific origins, the evolution of hardware, the greatest artists—including Tangerine Dream, Vangelis, Keith Emerson, Wendy Carlos, Jan Hammer, Kraftwerk, Brain Eno, Thomas Dolby, and others—in stories, interviews, illustrations, analysis, and practical musical technique. From the pages of *Keyboard* magazine, and with a foreword by Bob Moog.
ISBN 0-688-03106-4 $15.95   From Wm. Morrow & Co.

BEGINNING SYNTHESIZER

A step-by-step guide to understanding and playing synthesizers with discussions of how to use and edit presets and performance controls. A comprehensive, easy-to-understand, musical approach, with hands-on lessons in a variety of styles, including rock, pop, classical, jazz, techno-pop, blues, and more.
ISBN 0-88284-353-2 $12.95   From Alfred Publishing. Item Number 2606.

BEGINNING SYNTHESIZER is also available in a two-volume set of shorter Special Focus Guides, including:
Playing Synthesizers: A Beginners Guide To Effective Technique
ISBN 0-88284-362-1 $8.95   Item Number 4110.
Programming Synthesizers: A Beginner's Guide To Editing Preset Sounds
ISBN 0-88284-363-X $8.95   Item Number 4121.
All from Alfred Publishing.

MIND OVER MIDI

A comprehensive and practical introduction to this crucial new technology, including: What MIDI Does, Data Transmission Tutorial, Channels, Modes, Controllers, Computers, Interfaces, Software, Sequencers, Accessories, SMPTE & MIDI, MIDI systems, and more. Edited by Dominic Milano from the pages of *Keyboard* magazine.
ISBN 0-88188-551-7 $14.95   From Hal Leonard Publishing.

USING MIDI

The first comprehensive, practical guide to the application of Musical Instrument Digital Interface in performance, composition, and recording, including: basic MIDI theory, using MIDI performance controls, channels and modes, sequencers, MIDI synchronization, using MIDI effects, MIDI and computers, alternate MIDI controllers, and more. A definitive and essential tutorial.
ISBN 0-88282-354-0 $12.95   From Alfred Publishing. Item Number 2607.

USING MIDI is also available in a three-volume set of shorter Special Focus Guides, including:
What Is MIDI?: Basic Theory And Concepts
ISBN 0-88284-364-8 $8.95   Item Number 4126
Basic MIDI Applications: Sequencers, Drum Machines, And Keyboards
ISBN 0-88284-365-6 $8.95   Item Number 4139
Advanced MIDI Applications: Computers, Time Codes, And Beyond
ISBN 0-88284-365-6   Item Number 4143
All from Alfred Publishing.

BASIC GUITAR (Revised)

Chet Atkins, Arnie Berle, Paul Chasman, Dan Crary, Rik Emmett, Brad Gilis, Edward Van Halen, John Hammond, Bill Keith, Steve Morse, Arlen Roth, Mike Seeger, and other distinguished players and writers present a comprehensive, practical introduction to the technique and art of playing guitar. Edited from the pages of *Guitar Player* and *Frets* magazines by Helen Casabona, with a foreword by Les Paul.
ISBN 0-88188-906-7 $14.95   From Hal Leonard Publishing.

ROCK GUITAR

B.B. King, Lee Ritenour, Jeff Baxter, Larry Coryell, Arlen Roth, Rik Emmett, Jimmy Stewart, Bruce Bergman, Rick Derringer, Jim Aikin, and other outstanding working guitar players and teachers present a comprehensive approach to learning and performing the different styles of contemporary rock guitar. Edited by Jon Sievert from the pages of *Guitar Player* magazine.
ISBN 0-88188-294-1 $9.95   From Hal Leonard Publishing.

ELECTRIC BASS GUITAR

Carol Kaye, Chuck Rainey, Stanley Clarke, Herb Michman, Jeff Berlin, Michael Brooks, Andy West, Ken Smith, and other outstanding working bassists and bass teachers present a definitive approach to the theory, practice, and performance of electric bass guitar. Edited by Jon Sievert from the pages of *Guitar Player* magazine, with a foreword by Jeff Berlin.
ISBN 0-88188-292-5 $9.95   From Hal Leonard Publishing.

THE GUITAR PLAYER BOOK

The most comprehensive book on guitar ever produced, from the pages of America's foremost magazine for professional and amateur guitarists. Any style, any level, whether player or fan—this is the book. Includes definitive articles on all the important artists who have given the guitar its life and expression, plus design, instructions, equipment, accessories, and technique. Edited from the pages of *Guitar Player* magazine.
ISBN 0-394-62450-4 $11.95   From Grove Press

MULTI-TRACK RECORDING FOR MUSICIANS

How to make professional quality recordings at home or in the studio—comprehensive, creative practical information including basic theory and up-to-date guidance on the latest equipment.
ISBN 0-88284-355-9 $17.95   From Alfred Publishing. Item Number 2608.

To subscribe to *Keyboard*, *Guitar Player*, or *Frets*, write to magazine name, Subscription Department, P.O. Box 2110, Cupertino, CA 95015.

All prices subject to change without notice.